THE XXL UK KETO DIET COOKBOOK FOR BEGINNERS

1500 Days of Tasty, Quick and No-fuss Ketogenic Recipes to Start the Ketogenic

Diet and Lifestyle Full Colour Version

CONNIE J. CRANFORD

Table of Contents

While I have always been health-conscious most of my adult life, I have always shied away from extreme eating regimes. However, that all changed when I came across the ketogenic lifestyle. It was appealing enough on paper that I was willing to try it.

One reason I did was that despite my best efforts at the time, my waistline had been steadily growing. With my friend's big wedding fast approaching, I wanted to be sure I could comfortably fit into the bridesmaid's gown. Keto proved itself at the time, and I have been following it religiously. My mental alertness has grown significantly, and shedding weight is no longer the struggle it used to be.

Over the years, I have created unique, tasty recipes with ingredients you can easily find at your local food store. Below is a bit more about this awesome lifestyle choice.

Chapter 1
Basics of Ketosis

Recognizing the Signs of Ketosis

There are several signs that you may be in ketosis, although it can vary from person to person. Some common signs of ketosis include:

Increased thirst: When your body is in ketosis, it may produce more urine, which can lead to increased thirst.

Dry mouth: Ketosis can cause a decrease in saliva production, leading to a dry mouth.

Frequent urination: As mentioned, the body may produce more urine when in ketosis, leading to more frequent trips to the bathroom.

Bad breath: Ketosis can cause an unpleasant smell on the breath, often described as a fruity or metallic odor.

Increased focus and energy: Some people report increased mental clarity and energy when in ketosis.

Appetite suppression: Some people find that they are less hungry while in ketosis, although this can vary from person to person.

Weight loss: Many people following the ketogenic diet do experience weight loss, although this is not always the case.

It's important to note that these signs may not always be present, and they may not occur at the same time for everyone. It's also possible to be in ketosis without experiencing any of these signs. The most reliable way to confirm that you are in ketosis is to test your ketone levels using a ketone meter or test strips.

Test your Ketone Levels

There are several ways to test ketone levels:

Ketone strips: These are small strips of paper that you can use to test your urine for ketones. Simply urinate on the strip and wait for the color change to indicate the presence of ketones.

ketone meters: These are small devices that you can use to test your blood for ketones. They work by pricking your finger and collecting a small drop of blood, which is then placed on a test strip and inserted into the meter. The meter will then give you a reading of your ketone levels.

Breath analyzers: These devices test the levels of acetone, a type of ketone, in your breath.

It's important to note that the accuracy of these methods can vary, and they may not always give a completely accurate picture of your ketone levels. It's also important to follow the instructions for each method carefully to ensure accurate results.

Keto Flu

KETO FLUE SYMPTOMS

The "keto flu" is a term used to describe a group of symptoms that some people experience when they first start a ketogenic diet. These symptoms are thought to be caused by the body adjusting to the new diet and the lack of carbohydrates.

The symptoms of the keto flu can include:

Fatigue: Many people feel tired and sluggish when they first start a ketogenic diet.

Headaches: Some people experience headaches while in ketosis, possibly due to changes in electrolyte levels or dehydration.

Dizziness: Some people may feel lightheaded or dizzy while in ketosis.

Nausea: Some people may feel nauseous while in ketosis, possibly due to changes in their diet or the lack of carbohydrates.

Irritability: Some people may feel irritable or moody while in ketosis.

Insomnia: Some people may have difficulty sleeping while in ketosis.

These symptoms are usually temporary and typically resolve within a few days to a week. To help alleviate the symptoms of the keto flu, it is important to stay hydrated, get enough electrolytes, and eat enough protein. If the symptoms are severe or persist, it may be necessary to consult a healthcare professional.

THE KETO FLUE REMEDIES

There are several things you can do to help alleviate the symptoms of the keto flu:

Stay hydrated: It is important to drink plenty of water while on the ketogenic diet to help prevent dehydration.

Get enough electrolytes: The ketogenic diet can cause a loss of electrolytes, including sodium, potassium, and magnesium. To help prevent electrolyte imbalances, it is important to consume foods that are rich in these nutrients or consider taking supplements. Good sources of electrolytes include avocados, nuts, seeds, and leafy green vegetables.

Eat enough protein: It is important to eat enough protein on the ketogenic diet to support muscle mass and prevent muscle breakdown. Aim for around 20% of your daily calories to come from protein.

Get enough sleep: Getting enough sleep can help alleviate the fatigue that is common with the keto flu.

Take a break: If the symptoms of the keto flu are severe or persistent, it may be necessary to take a break from the diet and gradually reintroduce carbohydrates.

Getting into Ketosis

To get into ketosis, you will need to follow a ketogenic diet, which is a high-fat, low-carbohydrate diet. This means that you will need to drastically reduce your intake of carbohydrates and increase your intake of fats. Here are some steps you can take to get into ketosis:

Calculate your macros: Determine how many grams of fat, protein, and carbohydrates you should be eating each day to get into ketosis. A typical ketogenic diet consists of 75% fat, 20% protein, and 5% carbohydrates.

Reduce your carbohydrate intake: To get into ketosis, you will need to reduce your carbohydrate intake to a very low level, typically less than 50 grams per day. This means cutting out most sources of carbs, including bread, pasta, rice, and sugary foods.

Increase your fat intake: To make up for the calories you are no longer getting from carbohydrates, you will need to increase your fat intake. Good sources of healthy fats include olive oil, avocado, nuts, and seeds.

Eat enough protein: While the ketogenic diet is high in fat, it is important to eat enough protein to support your muscle mass. Aim for around 20% of your daily calories to come from protein.

Track your progress: Use a ketone meter or test strips to track your ketone levels and ensure that you are in ketosis. It can take a few days to a week for your body to enter ketosis, so be patient.

Chapter 2
Start your Keto Diet Journey

What is the Ketogenic Diet

The ketogenic diet is a high-fat, low-carbohydrate diet that has been shown to help some people lose weight. It involves dramatically reducing carbohydrate intake and replacing it with fat. This reduction in carbs puts your body into a metabolic state called ketosis, where fat, from your diet and from your body, is burned for energy.

The ketogenic diet is often used as a treatment for children with epilepsy who do not respond to other treatments, but it has also been suggested as a potential weight loss diet for adults. Some people claim that the diet can have a number of other health benefits, including improving insulin sensitivity, reducing inflammation, and possibly even reducing the risk of certain diseases such as cancer.

The Benefits of Entering Ketosis

There are several potential benefits to entering ketosis, although it is important to note that more research is needed to fully understand the effects of the ketogenic diet on the body. Some potential benefits of entering ketosis include:

Weight loss: Many people find that they lose weight on the ketogenic diet, although the exact mechanism is not fully understood. It is thought that the diet may help to reduce appetite, leading to fewer calories being consumed.

Improved insulin sensitivity: Some studies have shown that the ketogenic diet may improve insulin sensitivity, which can be beneficial for people with diabetes or at risk of developing diabetes.

Increased mental clarity: Some people report increased focus and mental clarity while in ketosis, although more research is needed to confirm this.

Reduced inflammation: The ketogenic diet may help to reduce inflammation in the body, which may be beneficial for people with certain conditions such as arthritis or asthma.

Reduced risk of certain diseases: Some research suggests that the ketogenic diet may be beneficial for reducing the risk of certain diseases, including cancer and Alzheimer's disease, although more research is needed to confirm this.

Once you make the switch to keto. Here are some of the benefits that will soon become apparent:

YOU WILL BEAT YOUR WEIGHT LOSS GOAL

A keto diet is a secret ingredient to weight loss for most people. You will likely surpass your goal of losing a few pounds in weeks. Most people who adhere to the diet find that they can effortlessly shed weight.

HIGHER ENERGY LEVELS

One side effect of eating processed foods is that your energy levels are often extremely low. After a day at the office, you will often feel spent, without the energy to interact with your friends and family. As you embrace the keto diet, you will start noticing that you have doubled or tripled your energy. For instance, you will find that you have the energy to go on short weekend trips instead of sleeping.

YOU MAKE MORE USE OF THE KITCHEN

With a keto diet, eating out at restaurants is almost impossible. While there are some specialized menu items, they are often not enough. A keto diet is an opportunity to get more in touch with your kitchen. It allows you to enjoy fresh meals every day that are made to your specifications.

The recipes in this cookbook are designed to be as simple as possible, taking little time to prepare. They are designed to make cooking a fun, enjoyable activity.

BREAK YOUR SUGAR ADDICTION

Processed sugar is everywhere these days. It is almost impossible to avoid it, and many people often have varying degrees of sugar addiction. With a keto diet, you will have to quit sugar. However, you will no longer have sugar cravings since you have an alternative energy source. While they will not go away on the first day, they will eventually dissipate.

Breaking a sugar addiction in the early stages is one of the best gifts you can give yourself. It ensures that for decades to come, you can enjoy optimal health.

Top 10 Keto Diet Benefits

Are you looking for fast, easy keto meals to help you lose weight? This cookbook has your back. Try the recipes below today!

1. Supports Metabolism
2. Blood Sugar Balance
3. Brain Health
4. Mental Focus
5. Uplifted Mood
6. Food Cravings
7. Heart Health
8. Energy Levels
9. Inflammation Response
10. Supports Hormone Balance

Week 1

Here is the following first week's meal plan for the keto diet. Try to follow the plan thoroughly to start getting the benefits of a keto diet.

Meal Plan	Breakfast	Snack	Lunch	Dinner	Snack
Day-1	Morning Veggies on Toast	Fried Garlic Calamari	Air-Fried Hot Wings	Cheese Burgers	Sage Muffins (2 servings)
	Calories: 243 | Total Fat: 10.3g | Carbs: 8.5g | Protein: 9.3g	Calories: 106 | Total Fat: 1.84g | Carbs: 8.42g | Protein: 12.86g	Calories: 296 | Total Fat: 11.9g | Carbs: 8.9g | Protein: 15.2g	Calories: 302 | Total Fat: 12.5g | Carbs: 12.2g | Protein: 16.2g	Calories: 85 | Fat: 8.3g | Fiber: 0.4g | Carbs: 0.9g | Protein: 1.4g
Day-2	Rice Paper Bacon	Crispy Cheese & Garlic Sticks	Chicken Meatballs	Meatballs with Sauce	Pecan Tarts
	Calories: 232 | Total Fat: 7.4g | Carbs: 6.2g | Protein: 7.3g	Calories: 143 | Total Fat: 8.4g | Carbs: 1.78g | Protein: 15.2g	Calories: 297 | Total Fat: 11.5g | Carbs: 9.3g | Protein: 14.8g	Calories: 302 | Total Fat: 12.3g | Carbs: 11.5g | Protein: 16.3g	Calories: 143 | Fat: 10.8g | Fiber: 5.7g | Carbs: 9.5g | Protein: 3.6g
Day-3	Air Fryer Broccoli & Tofu Scramble	Garlic Kale Chips (2 servings)	Hot Buffalo Chicken Wings	Spicy Beef Schnitzel	Chocolate Ice Pops (2 servings)
	Calories: 232 | Total Fat: 12.3g | Carbs: 5.6g | Protein: 14.5g	Calories: 50 | Total Fat: 1.9g | Carbs: 10g | Protein: 46g	Calories: 289 | Total Fat: 11.3g | Carbs: 8.7g | Protein: 15.2g	Calories: 306 | Total Fat: 12.6g | Carbs: 11.4g | Protein: 16.4g	Calories: 58 | Fat: 2.6g | Carbs: 5.5g | Protein: 3.1g | Fiber: 1.2g
Day-4	Paprika Zucchini Spread	Garlic Salmon Balls	Paprika Duck	Salmon Croquettes	Chocolate and Peanut Balls
	Calories: 240 | Fat: 14g | Fiber: 2g | Carbs: 5g | Protein: 11g	Calories: 219 | Total Fat: 7.7g | Carbs: 14.8g | Protein: 23.1g	Calories: 265 | Fat: 23.9g | Fiber: 0.1g | Carbs: 0.1g | Protein: 11.6g	Calories: 298 | Total Fat: 8.9g | Carbs: 7.6g | Protein: 15.2g	Calories: 328 | Fat: 32.6g | Carbs: 7.7g | Protein: 6.9g | Fiber: 2.7g
Day-5	Dill Egg Rolls	Roasted Vegetables with Paprika (2 servings)	Chili Chicken Cutlets	Salmon with Creamy Zucchini	Easy Everyday Brownies
	Calories: 81 | Fat: 4.4g | Fiber: 0.4g | Carbs: 5.7g | Protein: 4.9g	Calories: 80 | Total Fat: 6g | Carbs: 8g | Protein: 2g	Calories: 214 | Fat: 9g | Fiber: 0.2g | Carbs: 0.6g | Protein: 30.9g	Calories: 302 | Total Fat: 9.3g | Carbs: 7.8g | Protein: 15.7g	Calories: 123 | Fat: 12.9g | Carbs: 3.1g | Protein: 0.9g | Fiber: 1.7g

Day-6	Parsley Omelet	Garlic Eggplant Chips (2 servings)	Marinated Chicken	Grilled Salmon Fillets	Strawberry Almond Cake
	Calories: 240 | Fat: 13g | Fiber: 4g | Carbs: 6g | Protein: 9g	Calories: 61 | Fat: 3.7g | Fiber: 4.1g | Carbs: 7.2g | Protein: 1.2g	Calories: 254 | Fat: 14g | Fiber: 4g | Carbs: 6g | Protein: 15g	Calories: 302 | Total Fat: 8.6g | Carbs: 7.3g | Protein: 15.3g	Calories: 377 | Total Fat: 20.3g | Carbs: 43.3g | Protein: 5.8g
Day-7	Italian Breakfast Frittata	Cucumber Sushi	Tarragon Chicken Thighs	Indian Stewed Cabbage	Peach Cake
	Calories: 242 | Total Fat: 11.2g | Carbs: 9.3g | Protein: 12.3g	Calories: 114 | Fat: 8.7g | Fiber: 0.2g | Carbs: 1.4g | Protein: 7.4g	Calories: 437 | Fat: 17.3g | Fiber: 0.2g | Carbs: 0.4g | Protein: 65.8g	Calories: 235 | Fat: 17.7g | Carbs: 6.1g | Protein: 9.8g | Fiber: 2.4g	Calories: 317 | Total Fat: 13.1g | Carbs: 46.8g | Protein: 4.7g

Week 2

Here is the following second week's meal plan for a keto diet. It's the second stage of the 4 weeks meal plan that you must take into account carefully.

Meal Plan	Breakfast	Snack	Lunch	Dinner	Snack
Day-1	Air Fried Vegan Breakfast Bread	Hot Dogs	Curry Chicken Wings	Wrapped Pork	Fudge Bars with Almonds (2 servings)
	Calories: 252 | Total Fat: 9.6g | Carbs: 5.7g | Protein: 7.5g	Calories: 205 | Fat: 15.5g | Fiber: 4.1g | Carbs: 8g | Protein: 8.2g	Calories: 476 | Fat: 21.5g | Fiber: 0.3g | Carbs: 0.8g | Protein: 65.9g	Calories: 390 | Fat: 22.3g | Fiber: 0.2g | Carbs: 0.9g | Protein: 43.8g	Calories: 78 | Fat: 6.8g | Carbs: 4.7g | Protein: 0.5g | Fiber: 1g
Day-2	Dill Omelet	Coconut Salmon Bites (2 servings)	Creamed Chicken Breasts	Garlic Beef Steak	Grandma's Famous Cream Mousse
	Calories: 167 | Fat: 12.9g | Fiber: 0.4g | Carbs: 2g | Protein: 11.6g	Calories: 100 | Fat: 2g | Fiber: 1g | Carbs: 2g | Protein: 2g	Calories: 335 | Fat: 20.8g | Carbs: 4.3g | Protein: 30.9g | Fiber: 0.6g	Calories: 190 | Fat: 8.7g | Fiber: 0.1g | Carbs: 0.5g | Protein: 25.9g	Calories: 289 | Fat: 27.6g | Carbs: 5g | Protein: 5.9g | Fiber: 0g
Day-3	Garlic Zucchini Spread	Keto Mac&Cheese	Italian-Style Cocktail Meatballs	Cinnamon Ghee Pork Chops	Vanilla Shortcake
	Calories: 38 | Fat: 0.8g | Fiber: 2.4g | Carbs: 7.3g | Protein: 2.5g	Calories: 127 | Fat: 10.9g | Fiber: 1.5g | Carbs: 3.9g | Protein: 4.9g	Calories: 216 | Fat: 11.2g | Carbs: 3.6g | Protein: 24.3g | Fiber: 0.5g	Calories: 287 | Fat: 14g | Fiber: 4g | Carbs: 7g | Protein: 18g	Calories: 140 | Fat: 12.2g | Fiber: 1.1g | Carbs: 3.1g | Protein: 5.6g
Day-4	Soft Eggs	Chives Meatballs	Chinese Duck Breasts	Za'atar Beef Chops	Cheesy Orange Fritters
	Calories: 189 | Fat: 13.1g | Fiber: 0g | Carbs: 1g | Protein: 16.6g	Calories: 180 | Fat: 5g | Fiber: 2g | Carbs: 5g | Protein: 7g	Calories: 263 | Fat: 11.3g | Carbs: 3.7g | Protein: 34.4g | Fiber: 0.5g	Calories: 57 | Fat: 3.5g | Fiber: 0g | Carbs: 0.5g | Protein: 5.7g	Calories: 268 | Total Fat: 15.8g | Carbs: 25.8g | Protein: 6g
Day-5	Double Cheese and Sausage Balls	Eggplant Mash (2 servings)	Grilled Chicken Salad	Tomato Rib Eye Steaks	Chocolate Bread Pudding

	Calories: 412 | Fat: 34.6g | Carbs: 4.7g | Protein: 19.6g | Fiber: 0.1g	Calories: 83 | Fat: 1.6g | Fiber: 9.8g | Carbs: 16.4g | Protein: 3.7g	Calories: 403 | Fat: 18g | Carbs: 5.3g | Protein: 51.6g | Fiber: 1.6g	Calories: 943 | Fat: 75.8g | Fiber: 0.4g | Carbs: 1.2g | Protein: 60.5g	Calories: 482 | Total Fat: 22.9g | Carbs: 69.3g | Protein: 10.5g
Day-6	Party Cheese Ball with Herbs	Cheesy Asparagus (2 servings)	Creamy Pork Chops	Mustard Beef Loin	Baked Plum Dessert
	Calories: 176 | Fat: 15.7g | Carbs: 2g | Protein: 7.2g | Fiber: 0.9g	Calories: 49 | Fat: 2.3g | Fiber: 1.9g | Carbs: 3.7g | Protein: 4.9g	Calories: 303 | Fat: 25.6g | Fiber: 2.7g | Carbs: 5.5g | Protein: 15.1g	Calories: 492 | Fat: 23.8g | Fiber: 0.2g | Carbs: 0.3g | Protein: 69.5g	Calories: 198 | Total Fat: 9.3g | Carbs: 29.6g | Protein: 0.8g
Day-7	Dill Egg Rolls	Ranch and Blue Cheese Dip(2 servings)	Stuffed Beef Roll	Cumin, Chili & Squash	Bacon and Spinach Bowl
	Calories: 81 | Fat: 4.4g | Fiber: 0.4g | Carbs: 5.7g | Protein: 4.9g	Calories: 94 | Fat: 8.1g | Carbs: 1.3g | Protein: 0.1g | Fiber: 4.1g	Calories: 258 | Fat: 13.2g | Fiber: 0.6g | Carbs: 1.7g | Protein: 33.7g	Calories: 252 | Total Fat: 10.3g | Carbs: 7.6g | Protein: 8.7g	Calories: 215 | Fat: 16.1g | Fiber: 1.7g | Carbs: 4g | Protein: 15g

Week 3

Here is the following third week's meal plan for a keto diet. In this stage, you already got the result of the previous two weeks' diet plan. So, follow this third stage of the meal plan completely to get a better result.

Meal Plan	Breakfast	Snack	Lunch	Dinner	Snack
Day-1	Hard-Boiled Eggs	Peach Cake	Salmon and Lime Sauce	Mustard Beef Loin	Raspberry Jam (2 servings)
	Calories: 126 | Fat: 8.8g | Fiber: 0g | Carbs: 0.7g | Protein: 11.1g	Calories: 317 | Total Fat: 13.1g | Carbs: 46.8g | Protein: 4.7g	Calories: 227 | Fat: 12g | Fiber: 2g | Carbs: 4g | Protein: 9g	Calories: 492 | Fat: 23.8g | Fiber: 0.2g | Carbs: 0.3g | Protein: 69.5g	Calories: 9 | Fat: 0.1g | Fiber: 1.1g | Carbs: 2g | Protein: 0.2g
Day-2	Rice Paper Bacon	Grandma's Famous Cream Mousse	Garlic Beef Steak	Creamed Chicken Breasts	Crispy Cheese & Garlic Sticks
	Calories: 232 | Total Fat: 7.4g | Carbs: 6.2g | Protein: 7.3g	Calories: 289 | Fat: 27.6g | Carbs: 5g | Protein: 5.9g | Fiber: 0g	Calories: 190 | Fat: 8.7g | Fiber: 0.1g | Carbs: 0.5g | Protein: 25.9g	Calories: 335 | Fat: 20.8g Carbs: 4.3g | Protein: 30.9g | Fiber: 0.6g	Calories: 143 | Total Fat: 8.4g | Carbs: 1.78g | Protein: 15.2g
Day-3	Spinach Spread	Vanilla Shortcake	Catfish Bites	Italian-Style Cocktail Meatballs	Easy Everyday Brownies (2 servings)
	Calories: 200 | Fat: 4g | Fiber: 2g | Carbs: 4g | Protein: 4g	Calories: 140 | Fat: 12.2g | Fiber: 1.1g | Carbs: 3.1g | Protein: 5.6g	Calories: 187 | Fat: 11.3g | Fiber: 2.7g | Carbs: 4.4g | Protein: 16.5g	Calories: 216 | Fat: 11.2g | Carbs: 3.6g | Protein: 24.3g | Fiber: 0.5g	Calories: 123 | Fat: 12.9g | Carbs: 3.1g | Protein: 0.9g | Fiber: 1.7g
Day-4	Paprika Zucchini Spread	Peach Cake	Za'atar Beef Chops	Chili Chicken Cutlets	Garlic Salmon Balls
	Calories: 240 | Fat: 14g | Fiber: 2g | Carbs: 5g | Protein: 11g	Calories: 317 | Total Fat: 13.1g | Carbs: 46.8g | Protein: 4.7g	Calories: 57 | Fat: 3.5g | Fiber: 0g | Carbs: 0.5g | Protein: 5.7g	Calories: 214 | Fat: 9g | Fiber: 0.2g | Carbs: 0.6g | Protein: 30.9g	Calories: 219 | Total Fat: 7.7g | Carbs: 14.8g | Protein: 23.1g
Day-5	Cream Cheese Rolls	Chocolate Bread Pudding	Tomato Rib Eye Steaks	Grilled Chicken Salad	Eggplant Mash (2 servings)

	Calories: 85 | Fat: 6.7g | Fiber: 0g | Carbs: 0.5g | Protein: 5.9g	Calories: 482 | Total Fat: 22.9g | Carbs: 69.3g | Protein: 10.5g	Calories: 943 | Fat: 75.8g | Fiber: 0.4g | Carbs: 1.2g | Protein: 60.5g	Calories: 403 | Fat: 18g | Carbs: 5.3g | Protein: 51.6g | Fiber: 1.6g	Calories: 83 | Fat: 1.6g | Fiber: 9.8g | Carbs: 16.4g | Protein: 3.7g
Day-6	Parsley Omelet	Bacon and Spinach Bowl	Mustard Beef Loin	Cheesy Shrimps	Garlic Eggplant Chips (2 servings)
	Calories: 240 | Fat: 13g | Fiber: 4g | Carbs: 6g | Protein: 9g	Calories: 215 | Fat: 16.1g | Fiber: 1.7g | Carbs: 4g | Protein: 15g	Calories: 492 | Fat: 23.8g | Fiber: 0.2g | Carbs: 0.3g | Protein: 69.5g	Calories: 327 | Fat: 16.8g | Fiber: 3.9g | Carbs: 8.1g | Protein: 34.4g	Calories: 61 | Fat: 3.7g | Fiber: 4.1g | Carbs: 7.2g | Protein: 1.2g
Day-7	Omelet with Herbs de Provence	Bacon and Spinach Bowl	Cajun-Seasoned Lemon Salmon	Stuffed Beef Roll	Cheesy Asparagus (2 servings)
	Calories: 181 | Fat: 13.5g | Fiber: 0.1g | Carbs: 1.3g | Protein: 14.2g	Calories: 215 | Fat: 16.1g | Fiber: 1.7g | Carbs: 4g | Protein: 15g	Calories: 287 | Total Fat: 9.3g | Carbs: 8.4g | Protein: 15.3g	Calories: 258 | Fat: 13.2g | Fiber: 0.6g | Carbs: 1.7g | Protein: 33.7g	Calories: 49 | Fat: 2.3g | Fiber: 1.9g | Carbs: 3.7g | Protein: 4.9g

Week 4

This is the final stage of our 4 week's keto diet meal plan. In this stage, you already have formed a habit of maintaining a keto diet. So, follow this final stage to get best the best result in your body and mind.

Meal Plan	Breakfast	Snack	Lunch	Dinner	Snack
Day-1	Air Fried Vegan Breakfast Bread	Coconut Salmon Bites (2 servings)	Garlic Beef Steak	Pork Medallions with Cabbage	Hot Dogs
	Calories: 252 | Total Fat: 9.6g | Carbs: 5.7g | Protein: 7.5g	Calories: 100 | Fat: 2g | Fiber: 1g | Carbs: 2g | Protein: 2g	Calories: 190 | Fat: 8.7g | Fiber: 0.1g | Carbs: 0.5g | Protein: 25.9g	Calories: 528 | Fat: 31.8g | Carbs: 6.3g | Total Carbs: 51.2g | Fiber: 2.6g	Calories: 205 | Fat: 15.5g | Fiber: 4.1g | Carbs: 8g | Protein: 8.2g
Day-2	Parsley Omelet	Pecan Tarts	Cinnamon Ghee Pork Chops	Creamed Chicken Breasts	Eggplant Mash (2 servings)
	Calories: 240 | Fat: 13g | Fiber: 4g | Carbs: 6g | Protein: 9g	Calories: 143 | Fat: 10.8g | Fiber: 5.7g | Carbs: 9.5g | Protein: 3.6g	Calories: 287 | Fat: 14g | Fiber: 4g | Carbs: 7g | Protein: 18g	Calories: 335 | Fat: 20.8g | Carbs: 4.3g | Protein: 30.9g | Fiber: 0.6g	Calories: 83 | Fat: 1.6g | Fiber: 9.8g | Carbs: 16.4g | Protein: 3.7g
Day-3	Garlic Zucchini Spread	Chocolate Ice Pops (2 servings)	Cheesy Shrimps	Easy Spicy Meatballs	Keto Mac&Cheese
	Calories: 38 | Fat: 0.8g | Fiber: 2.4g | Carbs: 7.3g | Protein: 2.5g	Calories: 58 | Fat: 2.6g | Carbs: 5.5g | Protein: 3.1g | Fiber: 1.2g	Calories: 327 | Fat: 16.8g | Fiber: 3.9g | Carbs: 8.1g | Protein: 34.4g	Calories: 557 | Fat: 50.1g | Carbs: 2.3g | Total Carbs: 0.5g | Fiber: 0.9g	Calories: 127 | Fat: 10.9g | Fiber: 1.5g | Carbs: 3.9g | Protein: 4.9g
Day-4	Party Cheese Ball with Herbs	Keto Mac&Cheese	Stuffed Beef Roll	Chinese Duck Breasts	Cheesy Asparagus(2 servings)
	Calories: 176 | Fat: 15.7g | Carbs: 2g | Protein: 7.2g | Fiber: 0.9g	Calories: 127 | Fat: 10.9g | Fiber: 1.5g | Carbs: 3.9g | Protein: 4.9g	Calories: 258 | Fat: 13.2g | Fiber: 0.6g | Carbs: 1.7g | Protein: 33.7g	Calories: 263 | Fat: 11.3g | Carbs: 3.7g | Protein: 34.4g | Fiber: 0.5g	Calories: 49 | Fat: 2.3g | Fiber: 1.9g | Carbs: 3.7g | Protein: 4.9g
Day-5	Dill Egg Rolls	Easy Everyday Brownies	Garlic Beef Steak	Almond Broccoli and Chives	Eggplant Mash (2 servings)
	Calories: 81 | Fat: 4.4g | Fiber: 0.4g | Carbs: 5.7g | Protein: 4.9g	Calories: 123 | Fat: 12.9g | Carbs: 3.1g | Protein: 0.9g | Fiber: 1.7g	Calories: 190 | Fat: 8.7g | Fiber: 0.1g | Carbs: 0.5g | Protein: 25.9g	Calories: 180 | Fat: 4g | Fiber: 2g | Carbs: 4g | Protein: 6g	Calories: 83 | Fat: 1.6g | Fiber: 9.8g | Carbs: 16.4g | Protein: 3.7g

Day-6	Party Cheese Ball with Herbs	Chives Meatballs	Chicken Meatballs	Creamy Pork Chops	Cheesy Asparagus (2 servings)
	Calories: 176 | Fat: 15.7g | Carbs: 2g | Protein: 7.2g | Fiber: 0.9g	Calories: 180 | Fat: 5g | Fiber: 2g | Carbs: 5g | Protein: 7g	Calories: 297 | Total Fat: 11.5g | Carbs: 9.3g | Protein: 14.8g	Calories: 303 | Fat: 25.6g | Fiber: 2.7g | Carbs: 5.5g | Protein: 15.1g	Calories: 49 | Fat: 2.3g | Fiber: 1.9g | Carbs: 3.7g | Protein: 4.9g
Day-7	Dill Omelet	Peach Cake	Hot Buffalo Chicken Wings	Garlic Beef Steak	Peach Cake
	Calories: 167 | Fat: 12.9g | Fiber: 0.4g | Carbs: 2g | Protein: 11.6g	Calories: 317 | Total Fat: 13.1g | Carbs: 46.8g | Protein: 4.7g	Calories: 289 | Total Fat: 11.3g | Carbs: 8.7g | Protein: 15.2g	Calories: 190 | Fat: 8.7g | Fiber: 0.1g | Carbs: 0.5g | Protein: 25.9g	Calories: 317 | Total Fat: 13.1g | Carbs: 46.8g | Protein: 4.7g

Chapter 4
Breakfast

Morning Veggies on Toast

Prep Time: 2 minutes | Cook Time: 11 minutes | Serves 4

- 1 tablespoon olive oil
- ½ cup soft goat cheese
- 2 tablespoons softened butter
- 4 slices French bread
- 2 green onions, sliced
- 1 small yellow squash, sliced
- 1 cup button mushrooms, sliced
- 1 red bell pepper, cut into strips

1. Sprinkle your air fryer with olive oil and preheat it to 350˚Fahrenheit. Mix the red bell peppers, squash, mushrooms and green onions, cook them for 7-minutes.
2. Place vegetables on a plate and set aside. Spread the bread slices with butter and place into air fryer, with butter side up. Toast for 4-minutes.
3. Spread the goat cheese on toasted bread and top with veggies. Serve warm.

PER SERVING

Calories: 243 | Total Fat: 10.3g | Carbs: 8.5g | Protein: 9.3g

Rice Paper Bacon

Prep Time: 10 minutes | Cook Time: 30 minutes | Serves 4

- 4 pieces white rice paper,
- cut into 1-inch thick strips
- 2 tablespoons water
- 2 tablespoons liquid smoke
- 2 tablespoons cashew butter
- 3 tablespoons soy sauce or tamari

1. Preheat your air fryer to 350˚Fahrenheit. In a mixing bowl, add soy sauce, cashew butter, liquid smoke, and water, mix well. Soak the rice paper in this mixture for 5 minutes.
2. Place the rice paper in air fryer and do not overlap pieces. Air fry for 15-minutes or until crispy. Serve with steamed vegetables!

PER SERVING

Calories: 232 | Total Fat: 7.4g | Carbs: 6.2g | Protein: 7.3g

Air Fryer Broccoli & Tofu Scramble

Prep Time: 10 minutes | Cook Time: 30 minutes | Serves 3

- 4 cups broccoli florets
- 1 block tofu, chopped finely
- 2 ½ cups red potatoes, chopped
- 2 tablespoons olive oil
- 2 tablespoons tamari
- 1 teaspoon turmeric powder
- ½ teaspoon garlic powder
- ½ teaspoon onion powder
- ½ cup onion, chopped

1. Preheat your air fryer to 400°Fahrenheit. Mix the potatoes in a bowl with half of the olive oil. Place the potatoes into a baking dish that will fit into your air fryer and cook them for 15-minutes.
2. Combine the remaining olive oil, tofu, tamari, turmeric, garlic powder and onion powder. Stir in the chopped onions. Add the broccoli florets. Pour this mixture on top of the air-fried potatoes and cook for an additional 15-minutes. Serve warm.

PER SERVING

Calories: 232 | Total Fat: 12.3g | Carbs: 5.6g | Protein: 14.5g

Paprika Zucchini Spread

Prep Time: 5 minutes | Cook Time: 15 minutes | Serves 4

- 4 zucchinis, roughly chopped
- 1 tablespoon sweet paprika
- Salt and black pepper to the taste
- 1 tablespoon butter, melted

1. Grease a baking pan that fits the Air Fryer with the butter, add all the ingredients, toss, and cook at 360 degrees F for 15 minutes.
2. Transfer to a blender, pulse well, divide into bowls and serve for breakfast.

PER SERVING

Calories: 240 | Fat: 14g | Fiber: 2g | Carbs: 5g | Protein: 11g

Dill Egg Rolls

Prep Time: 10 minutes | Cook Time: 4 minutes | Serves 4

- 2 eggs, hard-boiled, peeled
- 1 tablespoon cream cheese
- 1 tablespoon fresh dill, chopped
- 1 teaspoon ground black pepper
- 4 wontons wrap
- 1 egg white, whisked
- 1 teaspoon sesame oil

1. Chop the eggs and mix them up with cream cheese, dill, and ground black pepper. Then place the egg mixture on the wonton wraps and roll them into the rolls. Brush every roll with whisked egg white.
2. After this, preheat the air fryer to 395F and brush the air fryer basket with sesame oil. Arrange the egg rolls in the hot air fryer and cook them for 2 minutes from each side or until the rolls are golden brown.

PER SERVING

Calories: 81 | Fat: 4.4g | Fiber: 0.4g | Carbs: 5.7g | Protein: 4.9g

Parsley Omelet

Prep Time: 5 minutes | Cook Time: 15 minutes | Serves 4

- 4 eggs, whisked
- 1 tablespoon parsley, chopped
- ½ teaspoons cheddar cheese, shredded
- 1 avocado, peeled, pitted and cubed
- Cooking spray

1. In a bowl, mix all the ingredients except the cooking spray and whisk well. Grease a baking pan that fits the Air Fryer with the cooking spray, pour the omelet mix, spread, introduce the pan in the machine and cook at 370 degrees F for 15 minutes.
2. Serve for breakfast.

PER SERVING

Calories: 240 | Fat: 13g | Fiber: 4g | Carbs: 6g | Protein: 9g

Italian Breakfast Frittata

Prep Time: 5 minutes | Cook Time: 10 minutes | Serves 2

- 4 cherry tomatoes, sliced into halves
- ½ Italian sausage, sliced
- ½ teaspoon Italian seasoning
- 3 eggs
- 2-ounces parmesan cheese, shredded
- 1 tablespoon parsley, chopped
- Salt and pepper to taste

1. Preheat your air fryer to 360°Fahrenheit. Put the sausage and cherry tomatoes into baking dish and cook for 5-minutes.
2. Crack eggs into small bowl, add parsley, Italian seasoning and mix well by whisking. Pour egg mixture over sausage and cherry tomatoes and place back into air fryer to cook for an additional 5-minutes. Serve warm.

PER SERVING

Calories: 242 | Total Fat: 11.2g | Carbs: 9.3g | Protein: 12.3g

Hard-Boiled Eggs

Prep Time: 8 minutes | Cook Time: 16 minutes | Serves 2

- 4 eggs
- ¼ teaspoon salt

1. Place the eggs in the air fryer and cook them for 16 minutes at 250F. When the eggs are cooked, cool them in the ice water.
2. After this, peel the eggs and cut into halves. Sprinkle the eggs with salt.

PER SERVING

Calories: 126 | Fat: 8.8g | Fiber: 0g | Carbs: 0.7g | Protein: 11.1g

Spinach Spread

Prep Time: 5 minutes | Cook Time: 10 minutes | Serves 4

- 2 tablespoons coconut cream
- 3 cups spinach leaves
- 2 tablespoons cilantro
- 2 tablespoons bacon, cooked and crumbled
- Salt and black pepper to the taste

1. In a pan that fits the air fryer, combine all the ingredients except the bacon, put the pan in the machine and cook at 360 degrees F for 10 minutes.
2. Transfer to a blender, pulse well, divide into bowls and serve with bacon sprinkled on top.

PER SERVING

Calories: 200 | Fat: 4g | Fiber: 2g | Carbs: 4g | Protein: 4g

Cream Cheese Rolls

Prep Time: 15 minutes | Cook Time: 10 minutes | Serves 4

- 4 eggs, beaten
- ½ teaspoon coconut oil, melted
- ½ teaspoon chili flakes
- 2 tablespoons cream cheese

1. Mix eggs with chili flakes.
2. Then brush the air fryer basket with coconut oil and preheat it to 395F.
3. Make 4 crepes from egg mixture and cook them in the air fryer basket.
4. Then spread the cream cheese over the every egg crepe and roll.

PER SERVING

Calories: 85 | Fat: 6.7g | Fiber: 0g | Carbs: 0.5g | Protein: 5.9g

Omelet with Herbs de Provence

Prep Time: 10 minutes | Cook Time: 18 minutes | Serves 3

- 6 eggs, beaten
- 1 tablespoon coconut milk
- 1 teaspoon Herbs de Provence
- 1 teaspoon coconut oil
- 1 oz Parmesan, grated

1. Grease the air fryer basket with coconut oil.
2. Mix eggs with coconut oil and Herbs de Provence. Pour the liquid in the air fryer.
3. Then top it with Parmesan and cook the meal at 365F for 18 minutes.

PER SERVING

Calories: 181 | Fat: 13.5g | Fiber: 0.1g | Carbs: 1.3g | Protein: 14.2g

Air Fried Vegan Breakfast Bread

Prep Time: 5 minutes | Cook Time: 10 minutes | Serves 2

- 1 vegan bread loaf, large
- 2 teaspoons chives
- 2 tablespoons nutritional yeast
- 2 tablespoons garlic puree
- 2 tablespoons olive oil
- Salt and pepper to taste

1. Preheat your air fryer to 375˚Fahrenheit. Slice the bread loaf (not all the way through).
2. In a bowl, combine the garlic puree, olive oil, and nutritional yeast. Add this mixture on top of the bread loaf. Sprinkle loaf with chives and season with salt and pepper. Place loaf inside of your air fryer and cook for 10-minutes.

PER SERVING

Calories: 252 | Total Fat: 9.6g | Carbs: 5.7g | Protein: 7.5g

Dill Omelet

Prep Time: 10 minutes | Cook Time: 15 minutes | Serves 4

- 8 eggs, beaten
- 1 tablespoon dill, dried
- ¼ cup of coconut milk
- ½ teaspoon coconut oil, melted

1. Mix eggs with dill and coconut milk.
2. Brush the air fryer basket with coconut oil and pour the egg mixture inside.
3. Cook the omelet for 15 minutes at 385F.

PER SERVING

Calories: 167 | Fat: 12.9g | Fiber: 0.4g | Carbs: 2g | Protein: 11.6g

Garlic Zucchini Spread

Prep Time: 10 minutes | Cook Time: 15 minutes | Serves 4

- 4 zucchinis, roughly chopped
- 1 teaspoon garlic powder
- 1 tablespoon avocado oil
- ½ teaspoon salt

1. Mix zucchini with garlic powder, avocado oil, and salt.
2. Put the mixture in the air fryer and bake at 375F for 15 minutes.
3. Then blend the cooked zucchini until you get smooth spread.

PER SERVING

Calories: 38 | Fat: 0.8g | Fiber: 2.4g | Carbs: 7.3g | Protein: 2.5g

Soft Eggs

Prep Time: 5 minutes | Cook Time: 16 minutes | Serves 2

- 6 eggs

1. Put the eggs in the air fryer basket and cook them at 250F for 16 minutes.
2. Serve.

PER SERVING

Calories: 189 | Fat: 13.1g | Fiber: 0g | Carbs: 1g | Protein: 16.6g

Double Cheese and Sausage Balls

Prep Time: 5 minutes | Cook Time: 20 minutes | Serves 3

- 1/2 pound breakfast sausage
- 1/2 cup almond flour
- 1/2 cup Colby cheese, shredded
- 4 tablespoons Romano cheese, freshly grated
- 1 egg
- garlic clove, pressed
- tablespoons fresh chives, minced

1. Thoroughly combine all ingredients in a mixing bowl; mix until everything is well incorporated.
2. Shape the mixture into balls and arrange them on a parchment-lined cookie sheet. Bake in the preheated oven at 360 degrees F for about 18 minutes.
3. Serve warm or cold. Bon appétit!

PER SERVING

Calories: 412 | Fat: 34.6g | Carbs: 4.7g | Protein: 19.6g | Fiber: 0.1g

Party Cheese Ball with Herbs

Prep Time: 5 minutes | Cook Time: 10 minutes plus chilling time | Serves 10

- 2 tablespoons mayonnaise
- 8 ounces extra-sharp cheddar cheese, shredded
- 6 ounces cream cheese, softened
- 1/2 cup sour cream
- 1/2 teaspoon paprika
- 1/4 teaspoon granulated garlic powder
- 1 teaspoon oregano
- 1 teaspoon basil
- 1 teaspoon rosemary
- teaspoon mint
- tablespoons chives, chopped

1. In a mixing bowl, thoroughly combine the mayonnaise, cheddar cheese, cream cheese, and sour cream until smooth and uniform.
2. Wrap the cheese mixture in a plastic wrap and form into a ball. Refrigerate the cheese ball at least 2 hours.
3. Meanwhile, mix the remaining ingredients until well combined. Roll the cheese ball over the herb mixture. Serve well chilled with assorted keto veggies. Bon appétit!

PER SERVING

Calories: 176 | Fat: 15.7g | Carbs: 2g | Protein: 7.2g | Fiber: 0.9g

Chapter 5
Snacks & Appetizers

Fried Garlic Calamari

Prep Time: 5 minutes | Cook Time: 10 minutes | Serves 4

- 1 lb. calamari, cut into rings
- ¼ cup of almond flour
- 1 cup pork rinds
- 3 mashed garlic cloves
- 2 large beaten eggs

1. Coat the calamari rings with flour. Dip the calamari in the mixture of the eggs and the mashed garlic. Dip them in the pork rinds. Cool the calamari rings in the fridge for 2-hours.
2. Then, put them into your air fryer and apply oil generously. Cook for 10-minutes at 380˚Fahrenheit.
3. Serve with garlic mayonnaise or lemon wedges.

PER SERVING

Calories: 106 | Total Fat: 1.84g | Carbs: 8.42g | Protein: 12.86g

Crispy Cheese & Garlic Sticks

Prep Time: 2 minutes | Cook Time: 4 minutes | Serves 4

- 1 cup almond flour
- 1 teaspoon garlic, minced
- ¼ teaspoon chili powder
- 1 teaspoon butter
- 3 cubes of cheddar cheese grated
- 1 teaspoon baking powder

1. Mix the flour and baking powder. Add the chili powder, garlic, salt, butter and grated cheese, along with a few drops of water. Make sure to make a stiff dough. Knead the dough for a while.
2. Now, sprinkle a small amount of flour on the counter. Take a rolling pin and roll the dough. Slice the dough into any shape you want. Preheat your air fryer to 370˚Fahrenheit. Set the time to 4-minutes and add cheese sticks to the basket. Serve with hot sauce!

PER SERVING

Calories: 143 | Total Fat: 8.4g | Carbs: 1.78g | Protein: 15.2g

Garlic Kale Chips

Prep Time: 5 minutes | Cook Time: 10 minutes | Serves 2

- 1 tablespoon yeast flakes
- Sea salt to taste
- 1 teaspoon vegan seasoning
- 4 cups packed kale
- 2 tablespoons olive oil
- 1 teaspoon garlic, minced

1. In a bowl, place the oil, the pieces of kale, garlic and the ranch seasoning. Add the yeast and mix well. Dump the coated kale into air fryer basket and cook at 375˚Fahrenheit for 5-minutes.
2. Shake after 3-minutes and serve.

PER SERVING

Calories: 50 | Total Fat: 1.9g | Carbs: 10g | Protein: 46g

Garlic Salmon Balls

Prep Time: 5 minutes | Cook Time: 15 minutes | Serves 2

- 6-ounces of tinned salmon
- 1 large egg
- 3 tablespoons olive oil
- 5 tablespoons wheat germ
- ½ teaspoon garlic powder
- 1 tablespoon dill, fresh, chopped
- 4 tablespoons spring onion, diced
- 4 tablespoons celery, diced

1. Preheat your air fryer to 370˚Fahrenheit. In a large bowl, mix the salmon, the egg, celery, onion, dill, and garlic. Shape the mixture into golf ball size balls and roll them in the wheat germ.
2. In a small pan, warm olive oil over medium-low heat. Add the salmon balls and slowly flatten them. Transfer them to your air fryer and cook for 10-minutes.

PER SERVING

Calories: 219 | Total Fat: 7.7g | Carbs: 14.8g | Protein: 23.1g

Roasted Vegetables with Paprika

Prep Time: 5 minutes | Cook Time: 10 minutes | Serves 4

- 1 lb. tomatoes
- 1 lb. green peppers
- 1 onion
- 3 cloves garlic
- 4 boiled eggs
- 1 tablespoon coriander powder
- 1 tablespoon lemon juice
- 2 -ounces of black olives
- Salt to taste
- 1 teaspoon paprika

1. Preheat your air fryer to 300°Fahrenheit. Line peppers, tomatoes, garlic, onion in the air fryer basket. Close lid and cook for 5-minutes, then flip veggies around and cook for another 5-minutes.
2. Remove veggies from air fryer and peel their skin. Place the veggies in a blender and sprinkle with salt, lemon juice, and coriander powder. Blend until smooth. Slice eggs in half. Divide veggie mixture up and top each plate with 1 boiled egg cut in half and sprinkle with paprika and drizzle with oil.

PER SERVING

Calories: 80 | Total Fat: 6g | Carbs: 8g | Protein: 2g

Garlic Eggplant Chips

Prep Time: 10 minutes | Cook Time: 25 minutes | Serves 4

- 1 eggplant, sliced
- 1 teaspoon garlic powder
- 1 tablespoon olive oil

1. Mix up olive oil and garlic powder. Then brush every eggplant slice with a garlic powder mixture.
2. Preheat the air fryer to 400F. Place the eggplant slices in the air fryer basket in one layer and cook them for 15 minutes. Then flip the eggplant slices on another side and cook for 10 minutes.

PER SERVING

Calories: 61 | Fat: 3.7g | Fiber: 4.1g | Carbs: 7.2g | Protein: 1.2g

Cucumber Sushi

Prep Time: 10 minutes | Cook Time: 10 minutes | Serves 10

- 10 bacon slices
- 2 tablespoons cream cheese
- 1 cucumber

1. Place the bacon slices in the air fryer in one layer and cook for 10 minutes at 400F.
2. Meanwhile, cut the cucumber into small wedges. When the bacon is cooked, cool it to the room temperature and spread with cream cheese. Then place the cucumber wedges over the cream cheese and roll the bacon into the sushi.

PER SERVING

Calories: 114 | Fat: 8.7g | Fiber: 0.2g | Carbs: 1.4g | Protein: 7.4g

Vegetable Roast

Prep Time: 5 minutes | Cook Time: 20 minutes | Serves 4

- 1 cup cauliflower, chopped
- 6 oz asparagus, chopped
- 1 tablespoon coconut oil
- 1 teaspoon Italian seasonings
- 1 teaspoon salt

1. Put all ingredients in the air fryer basket and shake well.
2. Cook the vegetables at 380F for 20 minutes. Stir them after 10 minutes of cooking.

PER SERVING

Calories: 48 | Fat: 3.8g | Fiber: 1.5g | Carbs: 3.1g | Protein: 1.4g

Garlic Chicken Meatballs

Prep Time: 5 minutes | Cook Time: 20 minutes | Serves 12

- 2 pound chicken breast, skinless, boneless and ground
- A pinch of salt and black pepper
- 2 garlic cloves, minced
- 2 spring onions, chopped
- 2 tablespoons ghee, melted
- 6 tablespoons keto hot sauce
- ¾ cup almond meal
- Cooking spray

1. In a bowl, mix all the ingredients except the cooking spray, stir well and shape medium meatballs out of this mix. Arrange the meatballs in your air fryer's basket, grease them with cooking spray and cook at 360 degrees F for 20 minutes.
2. Serve as an appetizer.

PER SERVING

Calories: 257 | Fat: 14g | Fiber: 1g | Carbs: 3g | Protein: 17g

Hot Dogs

Prep Time: 15 minutes | Cook Time: 5 minutes | Serves 4

- 4 hot dogs
- 1 egg, beaten
- 1/3 cup coconut flour
- ½ teaspoon ground turmeric

1. In the bowl mix up egg, coconut flour, and ground turmeric. Then dip the hot dogs in the mixture. Transfer the hot dogs in the freezer and freeze them for 5 minutes.
2. Meanwhile, preheat the air fryer to 400F. Place the frozen hot dogs in the air fryer basket and cook them for 6 minutes or until they are light brown.

PER SERVING

Calories: 205 | Fat: 15.5g | Fiber: 4.1g | Carbs: 8g | Protein: 8.2g

Coconut Salmon Bites

Prep Time: 5 minutes | Cook Time: 10 minutes | Serves 12

- 2 avocados, peeled, pitted and mashed
- 4 ounces smoked salmon, skinless, boneless and chopped
- 2 tablespoons coconut cream
- 1 teaspoon avocado oil
- 1 teaspoon dill, chopped
- A pinch of salt and black pepper

1. In a bowl, mix all the ingredients, stir well and shape medium balls out of this mix. Place them in your air fryer's basket and cook at 350 degrees F for 10 minutes.
2. Serve as an appetizer.

PER SERVING

Calories: 100 | Fat: 2g | Fiber: 1g | Carbs: 2g | Protein: 2g

Keto Mac&Cheese

Prep Time: 10 minutes | Cook Time: 10 minutes | Serves 4

- 2 cups cauliflower, chopped
- 1 teaspoon avocado oil
- 1 teaspoon salt
- 1 teaspoon dried oregano
- ½ cup Monterey Jack, shredded
- ½ cup of heavy cream
- ½ teaspoon coconut oil

1. Put the cauliflower in the air fryer basket.
2. Sprinkle it with avocado oil, salt, dried oregano, heavy cream, and coconut oil.
3. Then shake the mixture and top it with Monterey Jack cheese.
4. Cook the meal at 400F for 10 minutes.

PER SERVING

Calories: 127 | Fat: 10.9g | Fiber: 1.5g | Carbs: 3.9g | Protein: 4.9g

Chives Meatballs

Prep Time: 5 minutes | Cook Time: 20 minutes | Serves 6

- 1 pound beef meat, ground
- 1 teaspoon onion powder
- 1 teaspoon garlic powder
- A pinch of salt and black pepper
- 2 tablespoons chives, chopped
- Cooking spray

1. In a bowl, mix all the ingredients except the cooking spray, stir well and shape medium meatballs out of this mix.
2. Place them in your lined air fryer's basket, grease with cooking spray and cook at 360 degrees F for 20 minutes. Serve as an appetizer.

PER SERVING

Calories: 180 | Fat: 5g | Fiber: 2g | Carbs: 5g | Protein: 7g

Eggplant Mash

Prep Time: 10 minutes | Cook Time: 15 minutes | Serves 4

- ½ cup Mozzarella, shredded
- 2 eggplants, trimmed
- 1 tablespoon avocado oil
- ½ teaspoon dried cilantro

1. Chop the eggplants and sprinkle them with avocado oil.
2. Cook the vegetables in the air fryer for 15 minutes.
3. Then transfer them in the blender. Add cilantro and cheese.
4. Blend the mixture until smooth.

PER SERVING

Calories: 83 | Fat: 1.6g | Fiber: 9.8g | Carbs: 16.4g | Protein: 3.7g

Cheesy Asparagus

Prep Time: 10 minutes | Cook Time: 5 minutes | Serves 3

- 9 oz Asparagus
- 1 oz Parmesan, grated
- 1 teaspoon avocado oil

1. Chop the asparagus roughly and sprinkle with avocado oil.
2. Put it in the air fryer basket and cook at 400F for 5 minutes.
3. Then transfer the cooked asparagus in the serving plate and sprinkle with Parmesan.

PER SERVING

Calories: 49 | Fat: 2.3g | Fiber: 1.9g | Carbs: 3.7g | Protein: 4.9g

Lettuce Wraps with Ham and Cheese

Prep Time: 5 minutes | Cook Time: 10 minutes | Serves 5

- 10 Boston lettuce leaves, washed and rinsed well
- 1 tablespoon lemon juice, freshly squeezed
- 10 tablespoons cream cheese
- 10 thin ham slices
- 1 tomato, chopped
- 1 red chili pepper, chopped

1. Drizzle lemon juice over the lettuce leaves. Spread cream cheese over the lettuce leaves. Add a ham slice on each leaf.
2. Divide chopped tomatoes between the lettuce leaves. Top with chili peppers and arrange on a nice serving platter. Bon appétit!

PER SERVING

Calories: 148 | Fat: 10.2g | Carbs: 4.2g | Protein: 10.7g | Fiber: 0.8g

Ranch and Blue Cheese Dip

Prep Time: 5 minutes | Cook Time: 10 minutes | Serves 10

- 1/2 cup Greek-style yogurt
- 1 cup blue cheese, crumbled
- 1/2 cup mayonnaise
- 1 tablespoon lime juice
- Freshly ground black pepper, to taste
- 2 tablespoons ranch seasoning

1. In a mixing bowl, thoroughly combine all ingredients until well incorporated.
2. Serve well chilled with your favorite keto dippers. Bon appétit!

PER SERVING

Calories: 94 | Fat: 8.1g | Carbs: 1.3g | Protein: 0.1g | Fiber: 4.1g

Bacon and Spinach Bowl

Prep Time: 10 minutes | Cook Time: 6 minutes | Serves 2

- 2 cups spinach, chopped
- 1 oz bacon, chopped
- 1 pecan, chopped
- 1 teaspoon ground black pepper
- 2 oz Mozzarella, shredded

1. Put the bacon in the air fryer basket and cook at 400f for 6 minutes.
2. Then mix the cooked bacon with remaining ingredients.

PER SERVING

Calories: 215 | Fat: 16.1g | Fiber: 1.7g | Carbs: 4g | Protein: 15g

Greek-Style Ricotta Dip with Olives

Prep Time: 5 minutes | Cook Time: 15 minutes | Serves 8

- 10 ounces ricotta cheese
- 4 tablespoons Greek yogurt
- 1/2 teaspoon cayenne pepper
- 4 tablespoons olives, sliced
- 1/2 teaspoon shallot powder
- 1/2 teaspoon garlic salt
- 1/2 teaspoon black pepper
- 4 tablespoons cilantro, minced

1. Thoroughly combine the ricotta cheese, Greek yogurt, cayenne pepper, olives, shallot powder, garlic salt, and black pepper in a mixing bowl.
2. Transfer to a nice serving bowl.
3. Garnish with cilantro, serve and enjoy your party!

PER SERVING

Calories: 72 | Fat: 5.5g | Carbs: 1.9g | Protein: 4.3g | Fiber: 0.2g

Ranch Chicken Wings

Prep Time: 10 minutes | Cook Time: 55 minutes | Serves 6

- 2 pounds chicken wings, pat dry Nonstick cooking spray
- Sea salt and cayenne pepper, to taste Ranch Dressing:
- 1/4 cup sour cream
- 1/4 cup buttermilk
- 1/2 cup mayonnaise
- 1/2 teaspoon lemon juice
- 1 tablespoon fresh parsley, minced
- 1 clove garlic, minced
- 2 tablespoons onion, finely chopped
- 1/4 teaspoon dry mustard
- Sea salt and ground black pepper, to taste

1. Start by preheating your oven to 420 degrees F.
2. Spritz the chicken wings with a cooking spray. Sprinkle the chicken wings with salt and cayenne pepper. Arrange the chicken wings on a parchment-lined baking pan. Bake in the preheated oven for 50 minutes or until the wings are golden and crispy.
3. In the meantime, make the dressing by mixing all of the above ingredients. Serve with warm wings

PER SERVING

Calories: 466 | Fat: 37.2g | Carbs: 1.9g | Protein: 28.6g | Fiber: 0.1g

Colby Cheese-Stuffed Meatballs

Prep Time: 5 minutes | Cook Time: 25 minutes | Serves 8

- 1/2 pound ground pork 1 pound ground turkey
- 1 garlic clove, minced
- 4 tablespoons pork rinds, crushed
- 2 tablespoons shallots, chopped
- 4 ounces mozzarella string cheese, cubed
- 1 ripe tomato, pureed
- Salt and ground black pepper, to taste

1. In a mixing bowl, thoroughly combine all ingredients, except for the cheese. Shape the mixture into bite-sized balls.
2. Press 1 cheese cube into the center of each ball.
3. Place the meatballs on a parchment-lined baking sheet. Bake in the preheated oven at 350 degrees F for 18 to 25 minutes. Bon appétit!

PER SERVING

Calories: 389 | Fat: 31.3g | Carbs: 1.6g | Protein: 23.8g | Fiber: 0.5g

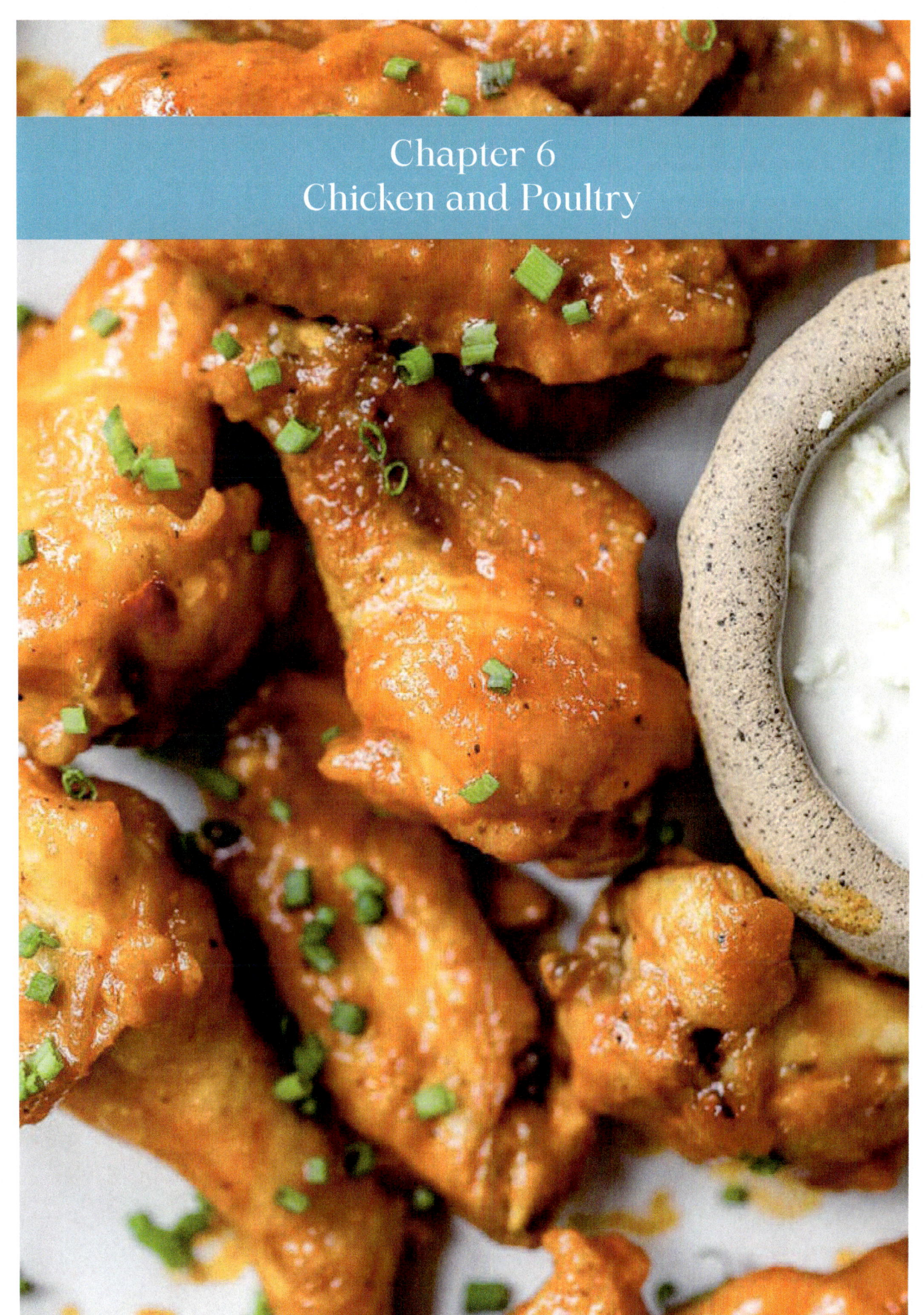

Chapter 6
Chicken and Poultry

Air-Fried Hot Wings

Prep Time: 5 minutes | Cook Time: 30 minutes | Serves 6

- 1 teaspoon liquid Stevia
- 1 tablespoon Worcestershire sauce
- ½ cup butter, melted
- 4 lbs. chicken wings
- ½ cup hot sauce
- ½ teaspoon salt

1. Add Stevia, Worcestershire sauce, butter, salt, and hot sauce in a bowl and mix well. Set aside.
2. Place chicken wings in air fryer basket and air fry at 380°Fahrenheit for 25-minutes. Shake basket halfway through. After 25-minutes, change the temperature to 400°Fahrenheit for 5-minutes. Add air-fried chicken wings into bowl mixture and toss well.

PER SERVING

Calories: 296 | Total Fat: 11.9g | Carbs: 8.9g | Protein: 15.2g

Chicken Meatballs

Prep Time: 5 minutes | Cook Time: 15 minutes | Serves 10

- 2 chicken breasts
- 1 tablespoon mustard powder
- Salt and pepper to taste
- 1 onion, diced
- 2 tablespoons honey
- 3 tablespoons soy sauce
- 1 teaspoon chili powder
- 1 tablespoon thyme
- 1 tablespoon basil
- 1 tablespoon cumin

1. Add chicken to food processor and process until minced. Add all the remaining ingredients into the food processor until combined.
2. Make small meatballs from the mixture and place them in air fryer basket. Air fry at 350°Fahrenheit for 15-minutes.

PER SERVING

Calories: 297 | Total Fat: 11.5g | Carbs: 9.3g | Protein: 14.8g

Air Fryer Chicken Cheese Zucchini Casserole

Prep Time: 20 minutes | Cook Time: 1 hour | Serves 8

- 2 lbs. ground chicken
- 2 (15-ounce) cans tomato sauce
- 1/8 teaspoon Stevia
- Salt and pepper to taste
- 1-pint ricotta cheese
- 2 zucchinis, cubed
- 3 eggs
- 2 tablespoons soy sauce
- ½ small onion, diced

1. Preheat your air fryer to 375°Fahrenheit and grease baking dish with olive oil.
2. In a bowl, add chicken, soy sauce, onion, and 2 eggs. Add ground chicken mixture to baking dish. Add zucchini on top.
3. In a bowl, mix egg, ricotta cheese, salt, and pepper. Add the cheese mixture on top of zucchinis.
4. In another bowl, mix stevia and tomato sauce. Add on top of cheese and bake in the air fryer for 1 hour.

PER SERVING

Calories: 289 | Total Fat: 11.8g | Carbs: 9.6g | Protein: 15.7g

Hot Buffalo Chicken Wings

Prep Time: 5 minutes | Cook Time: 22 minutes | Serves 3

- 2 lbs. chicken wings
- 1 cup buffalo sauce
- Salt and black pepper to taste

1. Wash and dry the chicken wings. Put into a bowl, and season with salt and pepper.
2. Preheat your air fryer to 380°Fahrenheit and cook the wings for 15-minutes. Put wings into a bowl of buffalo sauce and mix well.
3. Return to air fryer and cook for an additional 6-minutes.

PER SERVING

Calories: 289 | Total Fat: 11.3g | Carbs: 8.7g | Protein: 15.2g

Honey Lime Chicken Wings

Prep Time: 5 minutes | Cook Time: 12 minutes | Serves 2

- 16 chicken wings
- 2 tablespoons lime juice
- 2 tablespoons honey
- 2 tablespoons soy sauce
- Salt and pepper to taste

1. Mix the ingredients in a mixing bowl. Marinate the mix for 6-hours in the fridge.
2. Air-fry wings at 355°Fahrenheit for 6-minutes. Flip over chicken wings and cook for an additional 6-minutes.
3. Serve with a wedge of lemon.

PER SERVING

Calories: 286 | Total Fat: 11.6g | Carbs: 8.5g | Protein: 15.2g

Paprika Duck

Prep Time: 5 minutes | Cook Time: 28 minutes | Serves 6

- 10 oz duck skin
- 1 teaspoon sunflower oil
- ½ teaspoon salt
- ½ teaspoon ground paprika

1. Preheat the air fryer to 375F. Then sprinkle the duck skin with sunflower oil, salt, and ground paprika.
2. Put the duck skin in the air fryer and cook it for 18 minutes. Then flip it on another side and cook for 10 minutes more or until it is crunchy from both sides.

PER SERVING

Calories: 265 | Fat: 23.9g | Fiber: 0.1g | Carbs: 0.1g | Protein: 11.6g

Chili Chicken Cutlets

Prep Time: 20 minutes | Cook Time: 16 minutes | Serves 4

- 15 oz chicken fillet
- 1 teaspoon white pepper
- 1 teaspoon ghee, melted
- ½ teaspoon onion powder
- ¼ teaspoon chili flakes

1. Chop the chicken fillet into the tiny pieces. Then sprinkle the chopped chicken with white pepper, onion powder, and chili flakes. Stir the mixture until homogenous. Make the medium-size cutlets from the mixture.
2. Preheat the air fryer to 365F. Brush the air fryer basket with ghee and put the chicken cutlets inside. Cook them for 8 minutes and then flip on another side with the help of the spatula.
3. Transfer the cooked chicken cutlets on the serving plate.

PER SERVING

Calories: 214 | Fat: 9g | Fiber: 0.2g | Carbs: 0.6g | Protein: 30.9g

Marinated Chicken

Prep Time: 10 minutes | Cook Time: 30 minutes | Serves 4

- 1 and ½ cups Keto tomato sauce
- 1 teaspoon onion powder
- A pinch of salt and black pepper
- 1 tablespoon coconut aminos
- ½ teaspoon chili powder
- 2 pounds chicken drumsticks

1. In bowl, mix the chicken drumsticks with all the other ingredients, toss and keep in the fridge for 10 minutes.
2. Drain the drumsticks, put them in your air fryer's basket and cook at 380 degrees F for 15 minutes on each side. Divide everything between plates and serve.

PER SERVING

Calories: 254 | Fat: 14g | Fiber: 4g | Carbs: 6g | Protein: 15g

Apple Cider Vinegar Chicken Thighs

Prep Time: 10 minutes | Cook Time: 15 minutes | Serves 4

- 16 oz chicken thighs, skinless
- 1 teaspoon chili powder
- 1/3 cup apple cider vinegar
- 1 tablespoon avocado oil

1. Sprinkle the chicken thighs with chili powder, apple cider vinegar, and avocado oil.
2. Put them in the air fryer basket and cook at 380F for 15 minutes.

PER SERVING

Calories: 226 | Fat: 9g | Fiber: 0.4g | Carbs: 0.8g | Protein: 32.9g

Tarragon Chicken Thighs

Prep Time: 5 minutes | Cook Time: 30 minutes | Serves 4

- 2 pounds chicken thighs
- 1 tablespoon dried tarragon
- 1 tablespoon avocado oil
- ½ teaspoon salt

1. Mix chicken thighs with dried tarragon, avocado oil, and salt.
2. Put the chicken thighs in the air fryer basket and cook for 15 minutes per side at 360F.

PER SERVING

Calories: 437 | Fat: 17.3g | Fiber: 0.2g | Carbs: 0.4g | Protein: 65.8g

Chicken Tikka Masala

Prep Time: 10 minutes | Cook Time: 30 minutes | Serves 5

- 1½ pounds chicken breasts, cut into bite-sized pieces
- 1 onion, chopped
- 10 ounces tomato puree
- 1 teaspoon garam masala
- 1/2 cup heavy cream

1. Heat a wok that is greased with a nonstick cooking spray over medium-high heat. Now, sear the chicken breasts until golden brown on all sides.
2. Add the onions and sauté them for 2 to 3 minutes more or until tender and fragrant. Stir in the tomato puree and garam masala. Cook for 10 minutes until the sauce turns into a dark red color.
3. Fold in the heavy cream and stir to combine. Cook for 10 to 13 minutes more or until heated through.
4. Serve with cauliflower rice if desired and enjoy!

PER SERVING

Calories: 294 | Fat: 17.2g | Carbs: 4.6g | Protein: 29.3g | Fiber: 1.1g

Marinara Chicken Wings

Prep Time: 10 minutes | Cook Time: 30 minutes | Serves 5

- 3-pounds chicken wings
- ¼ cup marinara sauce
- 1 tablespoon coconut oil, melted

1. Mix marinara sauce with coconut oil.
2. Then put the chicken wings in the air fryer basket and add marinara sauce mixture.
3. Cook the meal at 360F for 30 minutes.

PER SERVING

Calories: 551 | Fat: 23.2g | Fiber: 0.3g | Carbs: 1.7g | Protein: 79g

Lemon Chicken Tenders

Prep Time: 5 minutes | Cook Time: 20 minutes | Serves 4

- 2-pounds chicken tenders
- 1 teaspoon lemon zest, grated
- 2 tablespoons lemon juice
- 1 tablespoon avocado oil

1. Mix avocado oil with lemon juice and lemon zest.
2. Then mix chicken tenders with lemon mixture and put in the air fryer.
3. Cook the chicken tenders at 365F for 10 minutes per side.

PER SERVING

Calories: 438 | Fat: 17.3g | Fiber: 0.2g | Carbs: 0.5g | Protein: 65.7g

Hot Chicken Wings

Prep Time: 5 minutes | Cook Time: 30 minutes | Serves 4

- 1 tablespoon olive oil
- 2 pounds chicken wings
- 1 tablespoon lime juice
- 2 teaspoons smoked paprika
- 1 teaspoon red pepper flakes, crushed
- Salt and black pepper to the taste

1. In a bowl, mix the chicken wings with all the other ingredients and toss well.
2. Put the chicken wings in your air fryer's basket and cook at 380 degrees F for 15 minutes on each side. Divide between plates and serve with a side salad.

PER SERVING

Calories: 280 | Fat: 13g | Fiber: 3g | Carbs: 6g | Protein: 14g

Splenda Chicken Wings

Prep Time: 15 minutes | Cook Time: 15 minutes | Serves 8

- 4-pounds chicken wings
- 1 tablespoon Splenda
- ½ teaspoon ground coriander

1. Rub the chicken wings with Splenda, avocado oil, and ground coriander.
2. Put the chicken wings in the air fryer basket and cook at 385F for 15 minutes.

PER SERVING

Calories: 441 | Fat: 17g | Fiber: 0.1g | Carbs: 1.6g | Protein: 65.6g

Mediterranean Chicken Drumettes

Prep Time: 10 minutes | Cook Time: 30 minutes | Serves 2

- 1 pound chicken drumettes
- 1 teaspoon Greek seasoning blend
- 1 tablespoon olive oil
- 6 ounces tomato sauce
- 6 Kalamata olives, pitted and sliced

1. Place the chicken drumettes and Greek seasoning blend in a Ziploc bag. Shake the bag, ensuring even coating.
2. Heat the olive oil in a saucepan over medium-high heat. Sear the chicken drumettes until golden brown, flipping them occasionally to ensure even cooking.
3. After that, stir in the tomato sauce and Kalamata olives. Continue to cook until the chicken is tender and everything is thoroughly heated or about 20 minutes. Bon appétit!

PER SERVING

Calories: 341 | Fat: 14.3g | Carbs: 3.6g | Protein: 47g | Fiber: 1.1g

Almond Coconut Chicken Tenders

Prep Time: 5 minutes | Cook Time: 20 minutes | Serves 4

- 4 chicken breasts, skinless, boneless and cut into tenders
- A pinch of salt and black pepper
- 1/3 cup almond flour
- 2 eggs, whisked
- 9 ounces coconut flakes

1. Season the chicken tenders with salt and pepper, dredge them in almond flour, then dip in eggs and roll in coconut flakes.
2. Put the chicken tenders in your air fryer's basket and cook at 400 degrees F for 10 minutes on each side. Divide between plates and serve with a side salad.

PER SERVING

Calories: 250 | Fat: 12g | Fiber: 4g | Carbs: 6g | Protein: 15g3

Curry Chicken Wings

Prep Time: 10 minutes | Cook Time: 25 minutes | Serves 4

- 2 pounds chicken wings, boneless
- 1 teaspoon curry powder
- 3 tablespoons heavy cream
- 1 tablespoon avocado oil

1. Mix heavy cream with curry powder.
2. Then mix chicken wings with curry mixture and put in the air fryer.
3. Sprinkle the chicken wings with avocado oil and cook them for 25 minutes at 375F.

PER SERVING

Calories: 476 | Fat: 21.5g | Fiber: 0.3g | Carbs: 0.8g | Protein: 65.9g

Creamed Chicken Breasts

Prep Time: 5 minutes | Cook Time: 15 minutes | Serves 4

- 1 tablespoon olive oil
- 1 yellow onion, chopped
- 2 garlic cloves, pressed
- 2 chicken breast, skinless and boneless, cut into bite-sized pieces
- 1/2 cup cream of mushroom soup

1. Heat the olive oil in a saucepan over medium-high heat. Once hot, sweat the yellow onion until tender and translucent about 3 minutes. Then, cook the garlic until aromatic or about 30 seconds.
2. Then, sear the chicken breast for 3 minutes, stirring frequently to ensure even cooking. Pour in the cream of mushroom soup and stir to combine.
3. Turn the heat to medium-low and let it simmer until the sauce has reduced by half or 6 to 8 minutes longer. Serve immediately.

PER SERVING

Calories: 335 | Fat: 20.8g | Carbs: 4.3g | Protein: 30.9g | Fiber: 0.6g

Italian-Style Cocktail Meatballs

Prep Time: 10 minutes | Cook Time: 25 minutes | Serves 4

- 1 pound ground turkey
- 1 tablespoon Italian seasoning blend
- 2 cloves garlic, minced
- 1/2 cup leeks, minced
- 1 egg

1. Throw all ingredients into a mixing bowl; mix to combine well.
2. Form the mixture into bite-sized balls and arrange them on a parchment-lined baking pan. Spritz the meatballs with cooking spray.
3. Bake in the preheated oven at 395 degrees F for 18 to 22 minutes. Serve with cocktail sticks and enjoy!

PER SERVING

Calories: 216 | Fat: 11.2g | Carbs: 3.6g | Protein: 24.3g | Fiber: 0.5g

Chinese Duck Breasts

Prep Time: 5 minutes | Cook Time: 25 minutes | Serves 4

- 1 ½ pounds duck breast 1 tablespoon sesame oil
- 1 white onion, chopped
- 1/4 cup rice wine
- 3 teaspoons soy sauce

1. Gently score the duck breast skin in a tight crosshatch pattern using a sharp knife.
2. Heat the sesame oil in a skillet over moderate heat. Now, sauté the onion until tender and translucent.
3. Add in the duck breasts; sear the duck breasts for 10 to 13 minutes or until the skin looks crispy with golden brown color; drain off the duck fat from the skillet.
4. Flip the breasts over and sear the other side for 3 minutes. Deglaze the skillet with rice wine, scraping up any brown bits stuck to the bottom. Transfer to a baking pan; add the rice wine and soy sauce to the baking pan.
5. Roast in the preheated oven at 400 degrees F for 4 minutes for medium-rare (140 degrees F), or 6 minutes for medium (155 degrees F).
6. Serve garnished with sesame seeds if desired. Enjoy!

PER SERVING

Calories: 263 | Fat: 11.3g | Carbs: 3.7g | Protein: 34.4g | Fiber: 0.5g

Grilled Chicken Salad

Prep Time: 5 minutes | Cook Time: 20 minutes | Serves 2

- 2 chicken breasts
- 2 tablespoons extra-virgin olive oil
- 4 tablespoons apple cider vinegar
- 1 cup grape tomatoes, halved
- 1 Lebanese cucumber, thinly sliced

1. Preheat your grill to medium-high temperature. Now, grill the chicken breasts for 5 to 7 minutes on each side.
2. Slice the chicken into strips and transfer them to a nice salad bowl. Toss with the olive oil, vinegar, grape tomatoes, and cucumber.
3. Garnish with fresh snipped chives if desired. Bon appétit!

PER SERVING

Calories: 403 | Fat: 18g | Carbs: 5.3g | Protein: 51.6g | Fiber: 1.6g

Chapter 7
Beef, Lamb and Pork

Cheese Burgers

Prep Time: 5 minutes | Cook Time: 11 minutes | Serves 6

- 1 lb. ground beef
- 6 slices cheddar cheese
- Salt and pepper to taste

1. Preheat the air fryer to 350°Fahrenheit. Season ground beef with pepper and salt. Make six patties from the mixture and place them into air fryer basket. Air fry patties for 10-minutes.
2. After 10-minutes, place cheese slices over patties and cook for another minute. Serve warm.

PER SERVING

Calories: 302 | Total Fat: 12.5g | Carbs: 12.2g | Protein: 16.2g

Meatballs with Sauce

Prep Time: 5 minutes | Cook Time: 12 minutes | Serves 8

- 1 lb. ground beef
- 1 egg, beaten
- 1 cup tomato sauce
- Salt and pepper to taste
- 1 small onion, minced
- ½ cup breadcrumbs
- 2 carrots, shredded
- ½ teaspoon garlic salt

1. Preheat air fryer to 400°Fahrenheit. Mix egg, carrots, breadcrumbs, onion, ground beef, garlic salt, salt, and pepper. Mix well. Make small meatballs out of mixture and place in the air fryer basket for 7 minutes.
2. Place meatballs in oven safe dish and pour tomato sauce over meatballs. Place the dish in the air fryer and cook at 320°Fahrenheit for 5-minutes. Serve warm.

PER SERVING

Calories: 302 | Total Fat: 12.3g | Carbs: 11.5g | Protein: 16.3g

Spicy Beef Schnitzel

Prep Time: 5 minutes | Cook Time: 12 minutes | Serves 4

- 4 thin beef schnitzels
- 2 tablespoons paprika
- 1 cup breadcrumbs
- 1 tablespoon sesame seeds
- 2 eggs, beaten
- 4 tablespoons almond flour
- 3 tablespoons olive oil
- Salt and pepper to taste

1. Preheat the air fryer to 350°Fahrenheit. Season schnitzel with pepper and salt.
2. In a bowl, mix the flour, salt, and paprika. In another bowl, mix breadcrumbs, olive oil, and sesame seeds. Add beaten eggs into a third bowl. Dip the schnitzel into flour mixture, then into the egg, and finally coat with breadcrumbs.
3. Place coated schnitzel in air fryer basket and cook for 12-minutes. Serve warm.

PER SERVING

Calories: 306 | Total Fat: 12.6g | Carbs: 11.4g | Protein: 16.4g

Marinated Beef & Broccoli

Prep Time: 5 minutes | Cook Time: 12 minutes | Serves 4

- 1 lb. broccoli, cut into florets
- ¾ lb. round steak, cut into strips
- 1 teaspoon of minced ginger
- 1 garlic clove, minced
- 1 tablespoon olive oil
- 1 teaspoon cornstarch
- 2 teaspoons sesame oil
- 1 teaspoon liquid stevia
- 1 teaspoon soy sauce
- 1/3 cup sherry wine
- 1/3 cup oyster sauce

1. Add stevia, soy sauce, sherry wine, cornstarch, sesame oil, oyster sauce into a mixing bowl and combine well. Add the steak strips into a bowl and mix well, then set aside for about 45-minutes.
2. Add your broccoli to the air fryer, then add the marinated steak on top of it and sprinkle ginger over the steak and broccoli mixture. Cook at 350°Fahrenheit for 12-minutes. Serve hot with some rice!

PER SERVING

Calories: 298 | Total Fat: 12.4g | Carbs: 11.2g | Protein: 16.2g

Stuffed Bell Peppers

Prep Time: 5 minutes | Cook Time: 23 minutes | Serves 4

- 1 small onion, chopped
- 2 garlic cloves, minced
- 1 lb. ground beef
- 1 teaspoon basil, dried
- 8-ounces tomato sauce
- 2 teaspoons Worcestershire sauce
- ½ cup rice, cooked
- 2/3 cup cheddar cheese, shredded
- 1 teaspoon garlic salt
- 1 teaspoon black pepper
- ½ teaspoon chili powder

1. Spray baking pan with cooking spray. In a pan add a bit of oil and saute onion and garlic over medium heat for 3-minutes.
2. Add the beef, basil, chili powder, garlic salt and black pepper into a saucepan and mix well. Cook for another 5-minutes or until meat is browned.
3. Remove the saucepan from heat. Add half of the cheese, Worcestershire sauce, rice, and tomato sauce into pan and mix. Stuff beef mixture into the four bell peppers. Preheat your air fryer to 400°Fahrenheit. Spray air fryer basket with cooking spray. Place the stuff bell peppers in the basket and cook for 11-minutes.
4. Top the bell peppers with the remaining cheese and cook for an additional 2-minutes. Serve hot!

PER SERVING

Calories: 305 | Total Fat: 12.6g | Carbs: 11.4g | Protein: 16.7g

Chili Tomato Pork

Prep Time: 15 minutes | Cook Time: 15 minutes | Serves 3

- 12 oz pork tenderloin
- 1 tablespoon grain mustard
- 1 tablespoon swerve
- 1 tablespoon keto tomato sauce
- 1 teaspoon chili pepper, grinded
- ¼ teaspoon garlic powder
- 1 tablespoon olive oil

1. In the mixing bowl mix up grain mustard, swerve, tomato sauce, chili pepper, garlic powder, and olive oil. Rub the pork tenderloin with mustard mixture generously and leave for 5-10 minutes to marinate.
2. Meanwhile, preheat the air fryer to 370F. Put the marinated pork tenderloin in the air fryer baking pan. Then insert the baking pan in the preheated air fryer and cook the meat for 15 minutes.
3. Cool the cooked meat to the room temperature and slice it into the servings.

PER SERVING

Calories: 212 | Fat: 9g | Fiber: 0.2g | Carbs: 6.4g | Protein: 29.8g

Pork and Asparagus

Prep Time: 5 minutes | Cook Time: 35 minutes | Serves 4

- 2 pounds pork loin, boneless and cubed
- ¾ cup beef stock
- 2 tablespoons olive oil
- 3 tablespoons keto tomato sauce
- 1 pound asparagus, trimmed and halved
- ½ tablespoon oregano, chopped
- Salt and black pepper to the taste

1. Heat up a pan that fits your air fryer with the oil over medium heat, add the pork, toss and brown for 5 minutes.
2. Add the rest of the ingredients, toss a bit, put the pan in the fryer and cook at 380 degrees F for 30 minutes. Divide everything between plates and serve.

PER SERVING

Calories: 287 | Fat: 13g | Fiber: 4g | Carbs: 6g | Protein: 18g

Creamy Pork Chops

Prep Time: 15 minutes | Cook Time: 10 minutes | Serves 4

- 2 pork chops
- ¼ cup coconut flakes
- 3 tablespoons almond flour
- ½ teaspoon salt
- ½ teaspoon dried parsley
- 1 egg, beaten
- 1 tablespoon heavy cream
- 1 teaspoon butter, melted

1. Cut every pork chops into 2 chops. Then sprinkle them with salt and dried parsley. After this, in the mixing bowl mix up coconut flakes and almond flour.
2. In the separated bowl mix up egg, heavy cream, and melted butter. Coat the pork chops in the almond flour mixture and them dip in the egg mixture. Repeat the same steps one more time. Then coat the pork chops in the remaining almond flour mixture.
3. Place the meat in the air fryer basket. Cook the pork chops for 10 minutes at 400F. Flip them on another side after 5 minutes of cooking.

PER SERVING

Calories: 303 | Fat: 25.6g | Fiber: 2.7g | Carbs: 5.5g | Protein: 15.1g

Stuffed Beef Roll

Prep Time: 20 minutes | Cook Time: 40 minutes | Serves 4

- pound beef loin
- 2 oz mushrooms, chopped
- 1 teaspoon onion powder
- 1 oz bacon, chopped, cooked
- ½ teaspoon dried dill
- 1 teaspoon chili powder
- 1 tablespoon avocado oil
- ½ teaspoon cream cheese

1. Beat the beef loin with the help of the kitchen hammer to get the flat loin.
2. After this, mix mushrooms with onion powder, bacon, dried dill, chili powder, and cream cheese.
3. Put the mixture over the beef loin and roll it.
4. Secure the beef roll with toothpicks and brush with avocado oil.
5. Cook the beef roll at 370F for 40 minutes.

PER SERVING

Calories: 258 | Fat: 13.2g | Fiber: 0.6g | Carbs: 1.7g | Protein: 33.7g

Wrapped Pork

Prep Time: 20 minutes | Cook Time: 16 minutes | Serves 2

- 8 oz pork tenderloin
- 4 bacon slices
- ½ teaspoon salt
- 1 teaspoon olive oil
- ½ teaspoon chili powder

1. Sprinkle the pork tenderloin with salt and chili powder. Then wrap it in the bacon slices and sprinkle with olive oil. Secure the bacon with toothpicks if needed.
2. After this, preheat the air fryer to 375F. Put the wrapped pork tenderloin in the air fryer and cook it for 7 minutes. After this, carefully flip the meat on another side and cook it for 9 minutes more.
3. When the meat is cooked, remove the toothpicks from it (if the toothpicks were used) and slice the meat.

PER SERVING

Calories: 390 | Fat: 22.3g | Fiber: 0.2g | Carbs: 0.9g | Protein: 43.8g

Pork Loin Steaks in Creamy Pepper Sauce

Prep Time: 5 minutes | Cook Time: 15 minutes | Serves 2

- 1 teaspoon lard, at room temperature
- 2 pork loin steaks
- 1/2 cup beef bone broth
- 2 bell peppers, deseeded and chopped
- 1 shallot, chopped
- 1 garlic clove, minced
- Sea salt, to season
- 1/2 teaspoon cayenne pepper
- 1/4 teaspoon paprika
- 1 teaspoon Italian seasoning mix
- 1/4 cup Greek-style yogurt

1. Melt the lard in a cast-iron skillet over moderate heat. Once hot, cook the pork loin steaks until slightly browned or approximately 5 minutes per side; reserve.
2. Add a splash of the beef bone broth to deglaze the pan. Now, cook the bell peppers, shallot, and garlic until tender and aromatic. Season with salt, cayenne pepper, paprika, and Italian seasoning mix.
3. After that, decrease the temperature to medium-low, add the Greek yogurt to the skillet and let it simmer for 2 minutes more or until heated through. Serve immediately.

PER SERVING

Calories: 447 | Fat: 19.2g | Carbs: 6g | Total Carbs: 62.2g | Fiber: 1.3g

Garlic Beef Steak

Prep Time: 10 minutes | Cook Time: 14 minutes | Serves 4

- 4 beef steaks
- 1 teaspoon garlic powder
- 1 tablespoon coconut oil

1. Mix beef steaks with garlic powder and coconut oil.
2. Put the beef steaks in the air fryer and cook them for 7 minutes per side at 400F.

PER SERVING

Calories: 190 | Fat: 8.7g | Fiber: 0.1g | Carbs: 0.5g | Protein: 25.9g

Cinnamon Ghee Pork Chops

Prep Time: 5 minutes | Cook Time: 35 minutes | Serves 4

- 4 pork chops, bone-in
- A pinch of salt and black pepper
- 2 and ½ tablespoons ghee, melted
- ½ teaspoon chipotle chili powder
- ½ teaspoon cinnamon powder
- ½ teaspoon garlic powder
- ½ teaspoon allspice
- 1 teaspoon coconut sugar

1. Rub the pork chops with all the other ingredients, put them in your air fryer's basket and cook at 380 degrees F for 35 minutes.
2. Divide the chops between plates and serve with a side salad.

PER SERVING

Calories: 287 | Fat: 14g | Fiber: 4g | Carbs: 7g | Protein: 18g

Pulled Pork with Mint and Cheese

Prep Time: 5 minutes | Cook Time: 20 minutes | Serves 2

- 1 teaspoon lard, melted at room temperature
- 3/4 pork Boston butt, sliced
- 2 garlic cloves, pressed
- 1/2 teaspoon red pepper flakes, crushed
- 1/2 teaspoon black peppercorns, freshly cracked
- Sea salt, to taste
- 2 bell peppers, deveined and sliced
- 1 tablespoon fresh mint leaves, snipped
- 4 tablespoons cream cheese

1. Melt the lard in a cast-iron skillet over a moderate flame. Once hot, brown the pork for 2 minutes per side until caramelized and crispy on the edges.
2. Reduce the temperature to medium-low and continue cooking another 4 minutes, turning over periodically. Shred the pork with two forks and return to the skillet.
3. Add the garlic, red pepper, black peppercorns, salt, and bell pepper and continue cooking for a further 2 minutes or until the peppers are just tender and fragrant.
4. Serve with fresh mint and a dollop of cream cheese. Enjoy!

PER SERVING

Calories: 370 | Fat: 21.9g | Carbs: 5.1g | Total Carbs: 34.9g | Fiber: 1g

Za'atar Beef Chops

Prep Time: 10 minutes | Cook Time: 11 minutes | Serves 6

- 6 beef chops
- 1 tablespoon coconut oil, melted
- 1 tablespoon za'atar seasonings

1. Mix za'atar seasonings with coconut oil.
2. Brush the beef chops with coconut oil mixture and put it in the air fryer.
3. Cook the meal at 400F for 11 minutes.

PER SERVING

Calories: 57 | Fat: 3.5g | Fiber: 0g | Carbs: 0.5g | Protein: 5.7g

Tomato Rib Eye Steaks

Prep Time: 10 minutes | Cook Time: 24 minutes | Serves 4

- 3-pound rib-eye steak
- 1 tablespoon keto tomato paste
- 1 tablespoon avocado oil
- 1 teaspoon salt
- 1 teaspoon cayenne pepper

1. In the shallow bowl, mix tomato paste with avocado oil, salt, and cayenne pepper.
2. Then run the beef with tomato mixture and put it in the air fryer.
3. Cook the meal at 380F for 12 minutes per side.

PER SERVING

Calories: 943 | Fat: 75.8g | Fiber: 0.4g | Carbs: 1.2g | Protein: 60.5g

Mustard Beef Loin

Prep Time: 10 minutes | Cook Time: 40 minutes | Serves 7

- 4-pounds beef loin
- 2 tablespoon Dijon mustard
- 1 tablespoon olive oil
- ½ tablespoon apple cider vinegar

1. Mix mustard with olive oil and apple cider vinegar.
2. Then rub the beef loin with mustard mixture and put it in the air fryer.
3. Cook the meal at 375F for 20 minutes per side.

PER SERVING

Calories: 492 | Fat: 23.8g | Fiber: 0.2g | Carbs: 0.3g | Protein: 69.5g

Pork Medallions with Cabbage

Prep Time: 5 minutes | Cook Time: 20 minutes | Serves 2

- 1 ounce bacon, diced
- 2 pork medallions
- 2 garlic cloves, sliced
- 1 red onion, chopped
- 1 jalapeno pepper, deseeded and chopped
- 1 tablespoon apple cider vinegar
- 1/2 cup chicken bone broth
- 1/3 pound red cabbage, shredded
- 1 bay leaf
- 1 sprig rosemary
- 1 sprig thyme
- Kosher salt and ground black pepper, to taste

1. Heat a Dutch pot over medium-high heat. Once hot, cook the bacon until it is crisp or about 3 minutes; reserve.
2. Now, cook the pork medallions in the bacon grease until they are browned on both sides.
3. Add the remaining ingredients and reduce the heat to medium-low. Let it cook for 13 minutes more, gently stirring periodically to ensure even cooking.
4. Taste and adjust the seasonings. Serve in individual bowls topped with the reserved fried bacon. Bon appétit!

PER SERVING

Calories: 528 | Fat: 31.8g | Carbs: 6.3g | Total Carbs: 51.2g | Fiber: 2.6g

Easy Spicy Meatballs

Prep Time: 5 minutes | Cook Time: 25 minutes | Serves 2

- 1 tablespoon ground flax seeds
- 2 ounces bacon rinds
- 1/2 pound ground pork
- 1 garlic clove, minced
- 1/2 cup scallions, chopped
- Sea salt and cayenne pepper, to taste
- 1/2 teaspoon smoked paprika
- 1/4 teaspoon ground cumin
- 1/4 teaspoon mustard seeds
- 1/2 teaspoon fennel seeds
- 1/2 teaspoon chili pepper flakes
- 2 tablespoons olive oil

1. In a mixing bowl, thoroughly combine all ingredients, except for the olive oil, until well combined. Form the mixture into balls and set aside.
2. Heat the olive oil in a nonstick skillet and fry the meatballs for about 15 minutes or until cooked through.
3. Serve with marinara sauce if desired. Bon appétit!

PER SERVING

Calories: 557 | Fat: 50.1g | Carbs: 2.3g | Total Carbs: 0.5g | Fiber: 0.9g

Chapter 8
Fish and Seafood

Salmon Croquettes

Prep Time: 5 minutes | Cook Time: 10 minutes | Serves 4

- 14-ounce tin of red salmon, drained
- 2 free-range eggs
- 5 tablespoons olive oil
- ½ cup breadcrumbs
- 2 tablespoons spring onions, chopped
- Salt and pepper to taste
- Pinch of herbs

1. Add drained salmon into a bowl and mash well. Break in the egg, add herbs, spring onions, salt, pepper and mix well.
2. In another bowl, combine breadcrumbs and oil and mix well. Take a spoon of the salmon mixture and shape it into a croquette shape in your hand. Roll it in the breadcrumbs and place inside air fryer. Set your air fryer to 390°Fahrenhiet for 10-minutes.

PER SERVING

Calories: 298 | Total Fat: 8.9g | Carbs: 7.6g | Protein: 15.2g

Salmon with Creamy Zucchini

Prep Time: 5 minutes | Cook Time: 10 minutes | Serves 2

- 2 (6-ounce) salmon fillets, skin on
- Salt and pepper to taste
- 1 teaspoon olive oil
- 2 large zucchinis, trimmed and spiralized
- 1 avocado, peeled and chopped
- Small handful of parsley, chopped
- ½ garlic clove, minced
- Small handful cherry tomatoes, halved
- Small handful of black olives, chopped
- 2 tablespoons pine nuts, toasted

1. Preheat your air fryer to 350°Fahrenheit. Brush salmon with olive oil and season with salt and pepper. Place salmon in air fryer and cook for 10-minutes.
2. Blend the avocado, garlic, and parsley in a food processor until smooth. Toss in a bowl with zucchini, olives, and tomatoes. Divide vegetables between two plates, top each portion with salmon fillet, sprinkle with pine nuts, and serve.

PER SERVING

Calories: 302 | Total Fat: 9.3g | Carbs: 7.8g | Protein: 15.7g

Grilled Salmon Fillets

Prep Time: 5 minutes | Cook Time: 8 minutes | Serves 2

- 2 salmon fillets
- 2 tablespoons olive oil
- 1 teaspoon liquid stevia
- 1/3 cup of light soy sauce
- 1/3 cup of water
- Salt and black pepper to taste

1. Season salmon fillets with salt and pepper. Whisk the rest of the ingredients in a bowl. Allow the salmon fillets to marinate in mixture for 2-hours.
2. Preheat your air fryer to 355°Fahrenheit for 5-minutes. Drain salmon fillets and air fry for 8-minutes.

PER SERVING

Calories: 302 | Total Fat: 8.6g | Carbs: 7.3g | Protein: 15.3g

Salmon Patties

Prep Time: 3 minutes | Cook Time: 10 minutes | Serves 2

- 3 large russet potatoes, boiled, mashed
- 1 salmon fillet
- 1 egg
- Breadcrumbs
- 2 tablespoons olive oil
- Parsley, fresh, chopped
- Handful of parboiled vegetables
- ½ teaspoon dill
- Salt and pepper to taste

1. Peel, chop, and mash cooked potatoes. Set aside.
2. Preheat your air fryer for 5-minutes at 355°Fahrenheit. Air fry salmon for five minutes. Use a fork to flake salmon then set aside.
3. Add vegetables, parsley, flaked salmon, dill, salt, and pepper to mashed potatoes. Add egg and combine. Shape the mixture into six patties. Cover with breadcrumbs. Cook in air fryer for 10-minutes.

PER SERVING

Calories: 297 | Total Fat: 8.5g | Carbs: 7.2g | Protein: 14.7g

Creamy Haddock

Prep Time: 10 minutes | Cook Time: 8 minutes | Serves 4

- pound haddock fillet
- 1 teaspoon cayenne pepper
- 1 teaspoon salt
- 1 teaspoon coconut oil
- ½ cup heavy cream

1. Grease the baking pan with coconut oil.
2. Then put haddock fillet inside and sprinkle it with cayenne pepper, salt, and heavy cream.
3. Put the baking pan in the air fryer basket and cook at 7375F for 8 minutes.

PER SERVING

Calories: 190 | Fat: 7.8g | Fiber: 0.1g | Carbs: 0.7g | Protein: 27.9g

Salmon and Lime Sauce

Prep Time: 5 minutes | Cook Time: 20 minutes | Serves 4

- 4 salmon fillets, boneless
- ¼ cup coconut cream
- 1 teaspoon lime zest, grated
- 1/3 cup heavy cream
- ¼ cup lime juice
- ½ cup coconut, shredded
- A pinch of salt and black pepper

1. In a bowl, mix all the ingredients except the salmon and whisk. Arrange the fish in a pan that fits your air fryer, drizzle the coconut sauce all over, put the pan in the machine and cook at 360 degrees F for 20 minutes.
2. Divide between plates and serve.

PER SERVING

Calories: 227 | Fat: 12g | Fiber: 2g | Carbs: 4g | Protein: 9g

Catfish Bites

Prep Time: 10 minutes | Cook Time: 10 minutes | Serves 4

- ¼ cup coconut flakes
- 3 tablespoons coconut flour
- 1 teaspoon salt
- 3 eggs, beaten
- 10 oz catfish fillet
- Cooking spray

1. Cut the catfish fillet on the small pieces (nuggets) and sprinkle with salt. After this, dip the catfish pieces in the egg and coat in the coconut flour. Then dip the fish pieces in the egg again and coat in the coconut flakes.
2. Preheat the air fryer to 385F. Place the catfish nuggets in the air fryer basket and cook them for 6 minutes. Then flip the nuggets on another side and cook them for 4 minutes more.

PER SERVING

Calories: 187 | Fat: 11.3g | Fiber: 2.7g | Carbs: 4.4g | Protein: 16.5g

Cheesy Shrimps

Prep Time: 15 minutes | Cook Time: 5 minutes | Serves 4

- 14 oz shrimps, peeled
- 2 eggs, beaten
- ¼ cup heavy cream
- 1 teaspoon salt
- 1 teaspoon ground black pepper
- 4 oz Monterey jack cheese, shredded
- 5 tablespoons coconut flour
- 1 tablespoon lemon juice, for garnish

1. In the mixing bowl mix up heavy cream, salt, and ground black pepper. Add eggs and whisk the mixture until homogenous. After this, mix up coconut flour and Monterey jack cheese. Dip the shrimps in the heavy cream mixture and coat in the coconut flour mixture. Then dip the shrimps in the egg mixture again and coat in the coconut flour.
2. Preheat the air fryer to 400F. Arrange the shrimps in the air fryer in one layer and cook them for 5 minutes. Repeat the same step with remaining shrimps. Sprinkle the bang-bang shrimps with lemon juice.

PER SERVING

Calories: 327 | Fat: 16.8g | Fiber: 3.9g | Carbs: 8.1g | Protein: 34.4g

Cajun-Seasoned Lemon Salmon

Prep Time: 2 minutes | Cook Time: 7 minutes | Serves 1

- 1 salmon fillet
- 1 teaspoon Cajun seasoning
- 2 lemon wedges, for serving
- 1 teaspoon liquid stevia
- ½ lemon, juiced

1. Preheat your air fryer to 350°Fahrenheit. Combine lemon juice and liquid stevia and coat salmon with this mixture. Sprinkle Cajun seasoning all over salmon. Place salmon on parchment paper in air fryer and cook for 7-minutes.
2. Serve with lemon wedges.

PER SERVING

Calories: 287 | Total Fat: 9.3g | Carbs: 8.4g | Protein: 15.3g

Mustard Cod

Prep Time: 10 minutes | Cook Time: 14 minutes | Serves 4

- 1 cup parmesan, grated
- 4 cod fillets, boneless
- Salt and black pepper to the taste
- 1 tablespoon mustard

1. In a bowl, mix the parmesan with salt, pepper and the mustard and stir. Spread this over the cod, arrange the fish in the air fryer's basket and cook at 370 degrees F for 7 minutes on each side.
2. Divide between plates and serve with a side salad.

PER SERVING

Calories: 270 | Fat: 14g | Fiber: 3g | Carbs: 5g | Protein: 12g

Turmeric Salmon

Prep Time: 10 minutes | Cook Time: 7 minutes | Serves 2

- 8 oz salmon fillet
- 2 tablespoons coconut flakes
- 1 tablespoon coconut cream
- ½ teaspoon salt
- ½ teaspoon ground turmeric
- ½ teaspoon onion powder
- 1 teaspoon nut oil

1. Cut the salmon fillet into halves and sprinkle with salt, ground turmeric, and onion powder. After this, dip the fish fillets in the coconut cream and coat in the coconut flakes. Sprinkle the salmon fillets with nut oil.
2. Preheat the air fryer to 380F. Arrange the salmon fillets in the air fryer basket and cook for 7 minutes.

PER SERVING

Calories: 209 | Fat: 12.8g | Fiber: 0.8g | Carbs: 0.2g | Protein: 22.4g

Jalapeno Cod

Prep Time: 5 minutes | Cook Time: 14 minutes | Serves 4

- 4 cod fillets, boneless
- 1 jalapeno, minced
- 1 tablespoon avocado oil
- ½ teaspoon minced garlic

1. In the shallow bowl, mix minced jalapeno, avocado oil, and minced garlic.
2. Put the cod fillets in the air fryer basket in one layer and top with minced jalapeno mixture.
3. Cook the fish at 365F for 7 minutes per side.

PER SERVING

Calories: 96 | Fat: 1.5g | Fiber: 0.3g | Carbs: 0.5g | Protein: 20.1g

Stuffed Mackerel

Prep Time: 15 minutes | Cook Time: 20 minutes | Serves 5

- pound mackerel, trimmed
- 1 bell pepper, chopped
- ½ cup spinach, chopped
- 1 tablespoon avocado oil
- 1 teaspoon ground black pepper
- 1 teaspoon keto tomato paste

1. In the mixing bowl, mix bell pepper with spinach, ground black pepper, and tomato paste.
2. Fill the mackerel with spinach mixture.
3. Then brush the fish with avocado oil and put it in the air fryer.
4. Cook the fish at 365F for 20 minutes.

PER SERVING

Calories: 252 | Fat: 16.6g | Fiber: 0.7g | Carbs: 0.5g | Protein: 22.1g

Indian Stewed Cabbage

Prep Time: 10 minutes | Cook Time: 30 minutes | Serves 3

- 6 ounces Goan chorizo sausage, sliced
- 2 cloves garlic, finely chopped
- 1 teaspoon Indian spice blend
- 1 pound white cabbage, outer leaves removed and finely shredded
- 3/4 cup cream of celery soup

1. Heat a large-sized wok over a moderate flame. Now, sear the Goan chorizo sausage until no longer pink; reserve.
2. Cook the garlic and Indian spice blend in the pan drippings until they are aromatic. Now, stir in the cabbage and cream of celery soup.
3. Turn the temperature to medium-low, cover, and continue simmering an additional 22 minutes or until tender and heated through.
4. Add the reserved Goan chorizo sausage; ladle into individual bowls and serve. Enjoy!

PER SERVING

Calories: 235 | Fat: 17.7g | Carbs: 6.1g | Protein: 9.8g | Fiber: 2.4g

Charred Broccoli Salad with Sardines

Prep Time: 5 minutes | Cook Time: 10 minutes | Serves 4

- 1 pound broccoli florets
- 1/2 white onion, thinly sliced
- 2 (4-ounce) cans sardines in oil, drained
- 2 tablespoons fresh lime juice
- 1 teaspoon stone-ground mustard

1. Heat a lightly greased cast-iron skillet over medium-high heat. Cook the broccoli florets for 5 to 6 minutes until charred; work in batches.
2. In salad bowls, place the charred broccoli with onion and sardines. Toss with the lime juice and mustard. Serve at room temperature. Bon appétit!

PER SERVING

Calories: 159 | Fat: 7.1g | Carbs: 5.7g | Protein: 17.8g | Fiber: 3g

Italian-Style Asparagus with Cheese

Prep Time: 5 minutes | Cook Time: 10 minutes | Serves 2

- 1/2 pound asparagus spears, trimmed, cut into bite-sized pieces
- 1 teaspoon Italian spice blend
- 1/2 tablespoon lemon juice
- 1 tablespoon extra-virgin olive oil
- 4 tablespoons Romano cheese, freshly grated

1. Bring a saucepan of lightly salted water to a boil. Turn the heat to medium-low. Add the asparagus spears and cook approximately 3 minutes. Drain and transfer to a serving bowl.
2. Add the Italian spice blend, lemon juice, and extra-virgin olive oil; toss until well coated.
3. Top with Romano cheese and serve immediately. Bon appétit!

PER SERVING

Calories: 193 | Fat: 14.1g | Carbs: 5.6g | Protein: 11.5g | Fiber: 2.4g

Sunday Cauliflower and Ham Bake

Prep Time: 5 minutes | Cook Time: 10 minutes | Serves 6

- 1 ½ pounds cauliflower, broken into small florets
- 1/2 cup Greek-Style yogurt
- 4 eggs, beaten
- 6 ounces ham, diced
- 1 cup Swiss cheese, preferably freshly grated

1. Place the cauliflower into a deep saucepan; cover with water and bring to a boil over high heat; immediately reduce the heat to medium-low.
2. Let it simmer, covered, approximately 6 minutes. Drain and mash with a potato masher.
3. Add in the yogurt, eggs and ham; stir until everything is well combined and incorporated.
4. Scrape the mixture into a lightly greased casserole dish. Top with the grated Swiss cheese and transfer to a preheated at 390 degrees F oven.
5. Bake for 15 to 20 minutes or until cheese bubbles and browns. Bon appétit!

PER SERVING

Calories: 236 | Fat: 13.8g | Carbs: 7.2g | Protein: 20.3g | Fiber: 2.3g

Squash Noodles

Prep Time: 20 minutes | Cook Time: 5 minutes | Serves 4

- 12 oz scallop squash
- 1 teaspoon butter, softened
- 1 oz Parmesan, grated
- 1 teaspoon sesame oil
- ¼ teaspoon cayenne pepper

1. Make the noodles from the scallop squash. Use the spiralizer for this step. Then place the vegetable noodles in the air fryer and sprinkle with sesame oil. Cook them for 5 minutes at 385F. Transfer the cooked noodles in the serving plates and sprinkle with butter and cayenne pepper. Then top the vegetables with Parmesan.

PER SERVING

Calories: 57 | Fat: 3.8g | Fiber: 0g | Carbs: 3.6g | Protein: 3.3g

Cumin, Chili & Squash

Prep Time: 5 minutes | Cook Time: 20 minutes | Serves 4

- 1 medium butternut squash
- 1 bunch coriander
- 2/3 cup Greek yogurt
- ¼ cup pine nuts
- 1 tablespoon olive oil
- 1 pinch chili flakes
- 2 teaspoons cumin seeds
- Salt and pepper to taste

1. Slice the squash into small chunks. Mix with the spices and oil in a baking pan. Roast the squash in your air fryer at 380°Fahrenheit for 20-minutes.
2. Toast the pine nuts and serve with Greek yogurt and sprinkle coriander on top.

PER SERVING

Calories: 252 | Total Fat: 10.3g | Carbs: 7.6g | Protein: 8.7g

Low-Carb Zucchini Roll-Ups

Prep Time: 5 minutes | Cook Time: 5 minutes | Serves 4

- 3 zucchinis, sliced thin, lengthwise
- Sea salt to taste
- 1 cup goat cheese
- ¼ teaspoon black pepper
- 1 tablespoon olive oil

1. Preheat air fryer to 390°Fahrenheit. Brush each zucchini strip with olive oil. Mix sea salt and black pepper with goat cheese. Spoon the goat cheese into the middle of each strip of zucchini and roll it up and fasten with a toothpick.
2. Place into air fryer and cook for 5-minutes.

PER SERVING

Calories: 243 | Total Fat: 8.7g | Carbs: 6.4g | Protein: 6.5g

Pineapple Sticks with Yogurt Dip

Prep Time: 5 minutes | Cook Time: 10 minutes | Serves 2

- ¼ cup dried coconut
- ½ pineapple
- 1 cup vanilla yogurt
- 1 sprig of fresh mint

1. Preheat your air fryer to 390°Fahrenheit. Cut the pineapple into sticks. Dip pineapple sticks into the dried coconut. Place the sticks covered with desiccated coconut into air fryer basket and cook for 10-minutes.
2. Prepare the yogurt dip. Dice the mint leaves and combine with vanilla yogurt and stir. Serve pineapple sticks with yogurt dip and enjoy!

PER SERVING

Calories: 246 | Total Fat: 8.4g | Carbs: 7.2g | Protein: 6.3g

Zucchini Fries & Roasted Garlic Aioli

Prep Time: 5 minutes | Cook Time: 12 minutes | Serves 4

- ½ cup mayonnaise
- Sea salt and pepper to taste
- 1 teaspoon roasted garlic, pureed
- 2 tablespoons olive oil
- ½ lemon, juiced
- Sea salt and pepper to taste
- ½ cup almond flour
- 2 eggs, beaten
- 1 cup breadcrumbs
- 1 large zucchini, cut into ½-inch sticks
- 1 tablespoon olive oil
- Cooking spray

1. Take three bowls and line them up on the counter. In the first, combine flour, salt, and pepper. Place eggs in the second bowl. Place breadcrumbs combined with salt and pepper in the third bowl. Take zucchini sticks and dip first into flour, then in the eggs, and then into crumbs. Preheat your air fryer to 400°Fahrenheit.
2. Cover sticks with cooking spray and layer in the basket. There should be two layers, pointing in opposite directions. Halfway through the 12-minute cook time rotate and turn the fries and spray with more cooking spray. Prepare the roasted garlic aioli in a medium bowl by mixing mayonnaise, pureed roasted garlic, olive oil and lemon juice. Stir in some pepper and salt. Serve the fries with the roasted garlic aioli and enjoy!

PER SERVING

Calories: 246 | Total Fat: 9.3g | Carbs: 8.1g | Protein: 7.4g

Parmesan Veggie Mix

Prep Time: 5 minutes | Cook Time: 15 minutes | Serves 4

- 1 broccoli head, florets separated
- ½ pound asparagus, trimmed
- Juice of 1 lime
- Salt and black pepper to the taste
- 3 tablespoons parmesan, grated

1. In a bowl, mix the asparagus with the broccoli and all the other ingredients except the parmesan, toss, transfer to your air fryer's basket and cook at 400 degrees F for 15 minutes.
2. Divide between plates, sprinkle the parmesan on top and serve.

PER SERVING

Calories: 172 | Fat: 5g | Fiber: 2g | Carbs: 4g | Protein: 9g

Garlicky Sautéed Kale

Prep Time: 5 minutes | Cook Time: 20 minutes | Serves 3

- 1/2 tablespoon olive oil
- 1 teaspoon fresh garlic, chopped
- 9 ounces kale, torn into pieces
- 1/2 cup Cottage cheese, creamed
- 1/2 teaspoon sea salt

1. Heat the olive oil in a saucepan over a moderate flame. Now, cook the garlic until just tender and aromatic.
2. Then, stir in the kale and continue to cook for about 10 minutes until all liquid evaporates.
3. Fold in the Cottage cheese and salt; stir until everything is heated through. Enjoy!

PER SERVING

Calories: 93 | Fat: 4.4g | Carbs: 6.1g | Protein: 7.1g | Fiber: 2.7g

Almond Broccoli and Chives

Prep Time: 5 minutes | Cook Time: 12 minutes | Serves 4

- 1 pound broccoli florets
- 3 garlic cloves, minced
- A pinch of salt and black pepper
- 3 tablespoons coconut oil, melted
- ½ cup almonds, chopped
- 1 tablespoon chives, chopped
- 2 tablespoons red vinegar

1. In a bowl, mix the broccoli with the garlic, salt, pepper, vinegar and the oil and toss. Put the broccoli in your air fryer's basket and cook at 380 degrees F for 12 minutes.
2. Divide between plates and serve with almonds and chives sprinkled on top.

PER SERVING

Calories: 180 | Fat: 4g | Fiber: 2g | Carbs: 4g | Protein: 6g

Cayenne Eggplant Puree

Prep Time: 15 minutes | Cook Time: 15 minutes | Serves 2

- 1 large eggplant, trimmed, peeled
- 1 teaspoon cayenne pepper
- ¼ cup chicken broth
- 1 garlic clove, peeled
- ½ teaspoon salt
- 1 teaspoon dried parsley
- ½ teaspoon avocado oil

1. Sprinkle the eggplant with salt and avocado oil. Put it in the air fryer and cook for 15 minutes at 390F. Then cool the cooked eggplant gently and chop roughly.
2. Transfer it in the blender. Add chicken broth, cayenne pepper, garlic, and dried parsley. Grind the mixture until it smooth. Transfer the cooked meal in the bowl.

PER SERVING

Calories: 69 | Fat: 0.9g | Fiber: 8.4g | Carbs: 14.7g | Protein: 3.1g

Chapter 10
Desserts and Staples

Sage Muffins

Prep Time: 10 minutes | Cook Time: 20 minutes | Serves 8

- 3 tablespoons coconut oil, softened
- 1 egg, beaten
- ½ cup Erythritol
- ¼ cup almond flour
- 1 teaspoon dried sage
- 3 tablespoons mascarpone
- ½ teaspoon baking soda
- Cooking spray

1. Spray the muffin molds with cooking spray.
2. Then mix all ingredients in the mixing bowl and stir until smooth.
3. Pour the mixture in the muffin molds and transfer in the air fryer.
4. Cook the muffins at 350F for 20 minutes.

PER SERVING

Calories: 85 | Fat: 8.3g | Fiber: 0.4g | Carbs: 0.9g | Protein: 1.4g

Pecan Tarts

Prep Time: 10 minutes | Cook Time: 10 minutes | Serves 5

- 3 pecans, chopped
- ½ cup coconut flour
- 1 egg, beaten
- 1 tablespoon coconut oil, softened
- 1 tablespoon swerve
- ½ teaspoon baking powder
- Cooking spray

1. Spray the air fryer basket with cooking spray.
2. Then mix coconut flour with egg, coconut oil, swerve, and baking powder.
3. When you get a smooth batter, pour it in the air fryer basket, flatten gently, and top with pecans.
4. Cook the tart at 375F for 10 minutes.

PER SERVING

Calories: 143 | Fat: 10.8g | Fiber: 5.7g | Carbs: 9.5g | Protein: 3.6g

Raspberry Cream

Prep Time: 10 minutes | Cook Time: 20 minutes | Serves 6

- ½ cup raspberries
- 1 tablespoon lime juice
- 2 tablespoons water
- 3 tablespoons Erythritol
- ¼ teaspoon ground cinnamon

1. Blend the raspberries and mix with lime juice, water, Erythritol, and ground cinnamon.
2. Pour the mixture in the air fryer and cook at 345F for 20 minutes.

PER SERVING

Calories: 6 | Fat: 0.1g | Fiber: 0.7g | Carbs: 1.5g | Protein: 0.1g

Chocolate and Peanut Balls

Prep Time: 10 minutes | Cook Time: 10 minutes plus freezing time | Serves 6

- 1/2 cup coconut oil
- 1/2 cup peanut butter, no sugar added
- 1/4 cup cocoa powder, unsweetened
- 1/4 cup Xylitol
- 4 tablespoons roasted peanuts, ground

1. Microwave the coconut oil until melted; add in the peanut butter and stir until well combined.
2. Add the cocoa powder and Xylitol to the batter. Transfer to your freezer for about 1 hour.
3. Shape the batter into bite-sized balls and roll them over the ground peanuts. Bon appétit!

PER SERVING

Calories: 328 | Fat: 32.6g | Carbs: 7.7g | Protein: 6.9g | Fiber: 2.7g

Chocolate Ice Pops

Prep Time: 10 minutes | Cook Time: 0 minutes plus freezing time | Serves 8

- 1 3/4 cups plain yogurt
- 4 tablespoons full-fat milk
- 5 tablespoons cocoa powder
- 1/2 teaspoon pure vanilla essence
- 3/4 cup Swerve

1. Place all ingredients in a bowl of your food processor.
2. Pour into popsicle molds and freeze. Bon appétit!

PER SERVING

Calories: 58 | Fat: 2.6g | Carbs: 5.5g | Protein: 3.1g | Fiber: 1.2g

Easy Everyday Brownies

Prep Time: 10 minutes | Cook Time: 20 minutes plus cooling time | Serves 10

- 1/2 cup butter, melted
- 1 ¼ cups coconut flour
- 1 teaspoon baking powder
- 1/3 cup cocoa powder, unsweetened
- 1 cup Xylitol

1. Mix all ingredients in the order listed above.
2. Scrape the batter into a parchment-lined baking pan.
3. Bake in the preheated oven at 360 degrees F approximately 20 minutes or until a tester comes out clean.
4. Transfer to a cooling rack for 1 hour before slicing and serving. Bon appétit!

PER SERVING

Calories: 123 | Fat: 12.9g | Carbs: 3.1g | Protein: 0.9g | Fiber: 1.7g

Strawberry Almond Cake

Prep Time: 5 minutes | Cook Time: 17 minutes | Serves 6

- 1/3 cup strawberry jam
- 1/3 cup almonds, slivered
- 3 eggs, beaten
- 1 stick butter
- 1/3 teaspoon baking powder
- 4-ounces coconut flour
- 1 tablespoon cornstarch (mix with flour)
- ½ teaspoon vanilla essence
- 1/3 teaspoon ground cinnamon
- 2 tablespoons Truvia for baking
- 1 teaspoon crystalized ginger
- Olive oil cooking spray

1. Lightly grease the cake pan with olive oil cooking spray. Now, whip the butter and Truvia using a blender. Fold in the eggs, almonds, and jam and beat again until well combined. Add flour, baking powder, vanilla essence, ginger and ground cinnamon.
2. Bake in preheated air-fryer at 310˚Fahrenheit for 17-minutes.

PER SERVING

Calories: 377 | Total Fat: 20.3g | Carbs: 43.3g | Protein: 5.8g

Peach Cake

Prep Time: 5 minutes | Cook Time: 35 minutes | Serves 6

- ½ lb. peaches, pitted and mashed
- ½ teaspoon baking powder
- 1 ¼ cups almond flour
- ½ teaspoon orange extract
- ¼ teaspoon nutmeg, freshly grated
- 2 eggs
- 2 tablespoons Truvia for baking
- ¼ teaspoon ground cinnamon
- 1 teaspoon pure vanilla extract

1. Preheat your air-fryer to 310˚Fahrenheit. Spritz the cake pan with olive oil cooking spray.
2. In a mixing bowl, beat the ghee with Truvia until creamy. Fold in the egg, mashed peaches and honey. Then, make the cake batter by mixing the remaining ingredients; now, stir in the peach mixture in with rest of ingredients.
3. Pour batter into cake pan and level the surface of batter. Bake 35-minutes and enjoy!

PER SERVING

Calories: 317 | Total Fat: 13.1g | Carbs: 46.8g | Protein: 4.7g

Raspberry Jam

Prep Time: 10 minutes | Cook Time: 20 minutes | Serves 12

- ¼ cup Erythritol
- 7 oz raspberries
- 1 tablespoon lime juice
- ¼ cup of water

1. Put all ingredients in the air fryer and stir gently.
2. Cook the jam at 350F for 20 minutes. Stir the jam every 5 minutes to avoid burning.

PER SERVING

Calories: 9 | Fat: 0.1g | Fiber: 1.1g | Carbs: 2g | Protein: 0.2g

Fudge Bars with Almonds

Prep Time: 5 minutes | Cook Time: 0 minutes | Serves 7

- 1 cup almonds
- 4 tablespoons coconut flakes
- 4 tablespoons cacao powder, no sugar added
- 3 tablespoons coconut oil
- 1/4 cup monk fruit powder

1. Process all ingredients in your blender until everything is well combined, scraping down the sides as needed.
2. Press firmly into a parchment lined rectangular pan.
3. Cut into squares and serve your bars well chilled. Bon appétit!

PER SERVING

Calories: 78 | Fat: 6.8g | Carbs: 4.7g | Protein: 0.5g | Fiber: 1g

Grandma's Famous Cream Mousse

Prep Time: 5 minutes | Cook Time: 5 minutes plus chilling time | Serves 4

- 2 cups double cream
- 4 egg yolks
- 1/2 teaspoon instant coffee
- 1 teaspoon pure coconut extract
- 6 tablespoons Xylitol

1. Heat the cream in a pan over low heat; let it cool slightly.
2. Then, whisk the egg yolks with the instant coffee, coconut extract, and Xylitol until well combined.
3. Add the egg mixture to the lukewarm cream. Warm the mixture over low heat until it has reduced and thickened.
4. Refrigerate for 3 hours before serving. Enjoy!

PER SERVING

Calories: 289 | Fat: 27.6g | Carbs: 5g | Protein: 5.9g | Fiber: 0g

Vanilla Shortcake

Prep Time: 15 minutes | Cook Time: 30 minutes | Serves 4

- 3 eggs, beaten
- ½ cup almond flour
- ½ teaspoon baking powder
- 2 teaspoons swerve
- 1 teaspoon vanilla extract
- ½ cup coconut cream
- Cooking spray

1. Spray the air fryer basket with cooking spray.
2. Then mix eggs with almond flour, baking powder, swerve, vanilla extract, and coconut cream.
3. When the mixture is smooth, pour it in the air fryer basket and flatten gently with the help of the spatula.
4. Cook the shortcake at 355F for 30 minutes.

PER SERVING

Calories: 140 | Fat: 12.2g | Fiber: 1.1g | Carbs: 3.1g | Protein: 5.6g

Cheesy Orange Fritters

Prep Time: 2 minutes | Cook Time: 4 minutes | Serves 8

- 1 ½ tablespoons orange juice
- ½ teaspoon ground star anise
- 1/3 teaspoon ground cinnamon
- 2 tablespoons Truvia for baking
- 1 ¼ cups almond flour
- 1 teaspoon vanilla extract
- ¾ cup whole milk
- 1 teaspoon orange rind, grated
- ¾ lb. cream cheese, at room temperature

1. Combine all the ingredients in a bowl. Next, drop teaspoons of the mixture into air-fryer cooking basket; air-fry for 4-minutes at 340˚Fahrenheit.

PER SERVING

Calories: 268 | Total Fat: 15.8g | Carbs: 25.8g | Protein: 6g

Chocolate Bread Pudding

Prep Time: 5 minutes | Cook Time: 35 minutes | Serves 6

- ¾ cup chocolate chips
- 2 eggs plus 1 egg yolk, beaten
- 1 teaspoon candied ginger
- 3 ½ tablespoons coconut oil, room temperature
- 2 tablespoons Truvia for baking
- 1/3 cup coconut milk creamer
- 8 slices ciabatta bread, cubed
- 2 teaspoons rum
- 1 cup soy milk

1. Place cubed bread into bowl. In another bowl, combine remaining ingredients, mix well. Scrape the chocolate mix into first dish with bread cubes. Allow to soak for 20-minutes.
2. Evenly divide the mixture between 2 mini loaf pans. Bake in air-fryer at 305˚Fahrenheit for 35-minutes.

PER SERVING

Calories: 482 | Total Fat: 22.9g | Carbs: 69.3g | Protein: 10.5g

Appendix 1 Measurement Conversion Chart

Volume Equivalents (Dry)

US STANDARD	METRIC (APPROXIMATE)
1/8 teaspoon	0.5 mL
1/4 teaspoon	1 mL
1/2 teaspoon	2 mL
3/4 teaspoon	4 mL
1 teaspoon	5 mL
1 tablespoon	15 mL
1/4 cup	59 mL
1/2 cup	118 mL
3/4 cup	177 mL
1 cup	235 mL
2 cups	475 mL
3 cups	700 mL
4 cups	1 L

Weight Equivalents

US STANDARD	METRIC (APPROXIMATE)
1 ounce	28 g
2 ounces	57 g
5 ounces	142 g
10 ounces	284 g
15 ounces	425 g
16 ounces (1 pound)	455 g
1.5 pounds	680 g
2 pounds	907 g

Volume Equivalents (Liquid)

US STANDARD	US STANDARD (OUNCES)	METRIC (APPROXIMATE)
2 tablespoons	1 fl.oz.	30 mL
1/4 cup	2 fl.oz.	60 mL
1/2 cup	4 fl.oz.	120 mL
1 cup	8 fl.oz.	240 mL
1 1/2 cup	12 fl.oz.	355 mL
2 cups or 1 pint	16 fl.oz.	475 mL
4 cups or 1 quart	32 fl.oz.	1 L
1 gallon	128 fl.oz.	4 L

Temperatures Equivalents

FAHRENHEIT(F)	CELSIUS(C) APPROXIMATE)
225 °F	107 °C
250 °F	120 ° °C
275 °F	135 °C
300 °F	150 °C
325 °F	160 °C
350 °F	180 °C
375 °F	190 °C
400 °F	205 °C
425 °F	220 °C
450 °F	235 °C
475 °F	245 °C
500 °F	260 °C

Appendix 2 The Dirty Dozen and Clean Fifteen

The Environmental Working Group (EWG) is a nonprofit, nonpartisan organization dedicated to protecting human health and the environment Its mission is to empower people to live healthier lives in a healthier environment. This organization publishes an annual list of the twelve kinds of produce, in sequence, that have the highest amount of pesticide residue-the Dirty Dozen-as well as a list of the fifteen kinds ofproduce that have the least amount of pesticide residue-the Clean Fifteen.

THE DIRTY DOZEN	
The 2016 Dirty Dozen includes the following produce. These are considered among the year's most important produce to buy organic:	
Strawberries	Spinach
Apples	Tomatoes
Nectarines	Bell peppers
Peaches	Cherry tomatoes
Celery	Cucumbers
Grapes	Kale/collard greens
Cherries	Hot peppers
The Dirty Dozen list contains two additional itemskale/collard greens and hot peppers-because they tend to contain trace levels of highly hazardous pesticides.	

THE CLEAN FIFTEEN	
The least critical to buy organically are the Clean Fifteen list. The following are on the 2016 list:	
Avocados	Papayas
Corn	Kiw
Pineapples	Eggplant
Cabbage	Honeydew
Sweet peas	Grapefruit
Onions	Cantaloupe
Asparagus	Cauliflower
Mangos	
Some of the sweet corn sold in the United States are made from genetically engineered (GE) seedstock. Buy organic varieties of these crops to avoid GE produce.	

Appendix 3 Index

CONNIE J. CRANFORD

Printed in Great Britain
by Amazon

24472958R00044